Help for
Billy

ALSO BY HEATHER T. FORBES

A Study Guide for Help for Billy

Beyond Consequences, Logic, and Control: Volume 1

Beyond Consequences, Logic, and Control: Volume 1
Spanish Edition

Beyond Consequences, Logic, and Control: Volume 1
Russian Edition

Beyond Consequences, Logic, and Control: Volume 2

Dare to Love

Help for *Billy*

A Beyond Consequences Approach to Helping Challenging Children in the Classroom

Heather T. Forbes, LCSW

Beyond Consequences Institute, LLC

BOULDER, COLORADO

Help for Billy

**A Beyond Consequences Approach
to Helping Challenging Children
in the Classroom**

Copyright © Heather Forbes, LCSW, 2012

Published by:
Beyond Consequences Institute, LLC
www.BeyondConsequences.com

ISBN: 978-0-9777040-9-5
Ebook ISBN: 978-0-9847155-4-1

Cover design by:
Bobbi Benson
Wild Ginger Press
www.WildGingerPress.com

Author photo by:
Haroon Ahmad
Chromatic Studios
www.ChromaticsStudio.com

TO KELLEY

Thank you for forever expanding my understanding of trauma. You have helped me to more deeply understand the world through the eyes and heart of pain, fear, overwhelm, and thus, of love.

Sistas always!

Check out the
Beyond Consequences Institute
website today to:

- Sign-up on our network and receive announcements of future free events such as webinars and lectures.

- Receive Heather's free eNewsletter for more Q&A support.

- Download free articles that will further your understanding of the Beyond Consequences Model.

- Learn how you can have Heather T. Forbes, LCSW in your area to hold a seminar or workshop.

- Purchase additional copies of this book for teachers, friends, and family members.

- View videos of how this model works when teachers and parents make the commitment to move from fear to love.

www.help-for-billy.com

and

www.beyondconsequences.com

Now Available:

A Study Guide for *Help for Billy*

Designed to help teachers go deeper into their
understanding of the concepts presented in *Help for Billy*,
this study guide provides an interactive tool to
bring the trauma-informed approach to life.

If you're a teacher or work in a school, this study guide will
help you lead a book study group. With this valuable
resource, you can get your entire school on the road
to implementing a trauma-informed platform!

For more information, log into:
www.BeyondConsequences.com

Contents

■

Part Two: The Beyond Consequences Classroom

A Note to the Reader

■

"Help for _____"

(Insert your child's name here.)

Insert in the space above the name of your child or student who is finding the classroom challenging. While this book's title reads "Help for Billy," it can also read "Help for Jessica" or "Help for Michael" or "Help for Brandon" or any other name that will make this book personal to your life.

Create your own custom title to this book so that it becomes very real for and applicable to the academic challenges you and your child or student face every day. School is supposed to be a wonderful experience for children, but for some children the exact opposite has become the norm.

School environments are designed for children who have their natural love for learning intact and for children whose systems are hardwired to be able to sit in a classroom and stay focused. But when a child comes along who does not fit this description, we have continued to expect this child to change and to fit into this predetermined mold, no matter how much he or she is unable.

In my work with parents and schools, I continually get the questions "Why can't this child be like the other kids?" and "Why can't he just sit and behave and be normal?"

These comparative questions are reflective of how the mind works. To make sense of our world and of specific situations in our lives, we compare. We naturally compare by size, shape, color, and other attributes. And we, unfortunately, do it with children, even though we have been advised by psychology experts not to compare children, not to compare siblings in a household, and to allow each child his individuality.

In my trainings, I began comparing "Child A" with "Child B" to show why these two children are so different. However, the labels Child A and Child B seemed so impersonal. We are talking about *real* children, children with hearts and souls who are precious and tender beyond this world. So instead of treating this comparison as a sterile scientific data exchange, I named the two children. Child A became "Andy" and Child B became "Billy." These two names were chosen because they can be gender neutral. Andy is short for both Andrew or Andrea. And we all are familiar with the famous female tennis player Billie Jean King, as well as Billy being short for William.

Andy is the child who fits the classic academic mold. Billy is the child who does not. This book is dedicated to giving understanding as to *why* Billy is different and what we can do to help him. It is not a book about how to make Billy be Andy.

This book will transform your entire paradigm about how we interact, support, and teach children like Billy—children who are square pegs we have been trying to force into round holes for far too long.

Help for Billy is designed for both parents and educators. There is not a separate book for parents and a separate book for educators. It's the same book. We are all working with the same child. Thus, it is our responsibility to Billy to all work on the same team with the same understanding to best support him congruently.

The basis for the approach that I lay out in the following pages comes from the scientific evidence we now have regarding Billy and from the basic understanding of human needs. Yet, more importantly, it comes from the eyes and heart of Billy.

To truly understand someone, it takes a willingness to see life from the other person's perspective; it takes getting outside of ourselves and our familiar reality. It takes courage to step into the other person's world. That is how solutions that truly work can be formulated and that is where the chance to change a child's academic failures to academic successes resides.

I invite you to read this book to discover how to find *Help for [Your Child's Name]* and expand yourself into a brand new reality. Go beyond consequences, logic, and control and have fun seeing the world of your child from a whole new light and understanding!

Press on,
Heather T. Forbes, LCSW

PART ONE

Creating a
New Understanding

CHAPTER ONE

Ask the Experts

∎

If the only tool you have is a hammer,
you tend to see every problem as a nail.
~ Abraham Maslow

When kindergarteners get fired from kindergarten, we have a serious problem in our perspective of childhood behavior. The solutions that are traditionally in place for children with challenging, difficult, and even severe behaviors are not working—they are failing our children in the classroom. Or more importantly, *we* are failing our children in the classroom. Continuing to see every problem as a "nail," as suggested in the opening quote above, is where we need to begin.

If the only tool we have is a hammer, then we must add more tools to the toolbox. In other words, we must step back and broaden our perspective of children and understand what their behaviors are indicating. We must be willing to step back and see things differently and be willing to try something new that is unfamiliar and in many cases counter to that of tradition.

We live in a world that is different than it was fifty years ago, even twenty years ago. As a result, we are teaching different children in the classroom than in the past. Additionally, neuroscience has advanced remarkably to give us a deeper understanding of the brain. When we can understand the brain, we can understand our children because of this basic concept: The brain drives behavior.[1]

Another resource, largely untapped, that provides a deeper understanding of our children is ... our children! Why not ask our children what they need in the classroom? After all, they are the experts because they are the ones sitting in the classroom experiencing the academic environments we have created.

The fear in us as adults says that our children will ask for silly things or make unrealistic demands when it comes to improving their educational experience. Our adult minds think they will make comments like, "I want a cupcake on my desk every day when I arrive at school" or "I think every desk should have its own personal TV and Xbox."

Nothing could be further from the truth. Our children *do* know what they need. They are insightful and they have a natural love for learning that should be honored and respected. Far too often we make life too complicated and we miss the obvious solutions that are simple and effective, many of which are right in front of us; it is just that we are looking from the perspective of the "hammer."

Survey. A survey was created by the Beyond Consequences Institute (BCI) to ask the opinions of our expert children. The families on the BCI email network were invited to participate in this online survey on a volunteer basis. The survey was completed mainly by the students for whom this book was written (students who are unresponsive or even reactive to traditional methods of teaching and discipline), as the majority of families on this network include such students.

Children ranging from first to twelfth grade completed the survey. The responses were profoundly simple yet deeply insightful. They were also congruent with and supported the concepts in this book. The main question asked in this survey was:

> **"What do children need at school to make learning better? In other words, what would make you look forward to getting up and going to school every day?"**

What the "Experts" Need. Each participant was given space to type in three responses to this one question. The most frequently mentioned responses fell into four main categories: (1) less stress and less overwhelm, (2) better teacher-student relationships, (3) better peer relations, and (4) more fun.

1. 14% of the responses gave suggestions for decreasing the level of stress and overwhelm:
    *   *"Less students and more one on one with teacher"*

- *"It would help if there weren't so many kids in the class"*
- *"Keeping things the same on set days"*
- *"Feel better when teacher is there with me, more help"*
- *"Smaller groups in each class"*
- *"More breaks throughout the class"*

2. 12% of the responses gave suggestions for improvements in the types of teachers as well as the teacher-student relationship:
   - *"A nice teacher"*
   - *"Teachers who get more involved with the students"*
   - *"It would help if the teacher was nicer and wouldn't yell at kids so much"*
   - *"Kind teachers"*
   - *"Teachers with a nice voice, even when you make them upset they stay calm and have a calm voice"*
   - *"Have kind teachers who help me"*
   - *"A teacher who would walk around the class engaging with all the kids!"*

3. 10% of the responses reflected the importance of positive peer relations and the importance of friends:
   - *"If I had more friends"*
   - *"Teachers be aware of kids bullying and not being afraid to interact and do something"*
   - *"Meeting new friends"*
   - *"A place where everybody's accepting of everybody's differences and maybe challenges"*
   - *"Knowing that my friends are there to back me up if I need help with something"*
   - *"Make kids stop bullying me"*
   - *"Teachers should make people feel good in class and not bullied"*

4. 10% of the responses had the word "fun" included:
   - *"Make math class fun by using games to teach"*
   - *"Fun activities in classes"*
   - *"That you know you have a fun teacher"*

- *"Making school work fun"*
- *"Putting lessons into fun games"*
- *"Play some fun learning games and then take a break and play a regular game"*
- *"If classes were more fun and interesting"*

Another question given was reflective in nature, asking the student to give insight into the past school year:

"Did you like school this past year? Why or why not?"

- *"Yes, because I had the best teacher ever and she helped my class become a family."*
- *"Yes, because my teacher was very nice."*
- *"Yes I did. Because I got long recesses."*
- *"Yes. We had games in between lessons."*
- *"No because of bullies!"*
- *"No. I got bullied and sent out of the classroom all the time. One time I didn't want to leave the classroom and be in the hallway alone so I knocked a chair over and wouldn't go. My teacher didn't like me after that and said I was emotionally impaired."*
- *"BIG FAT NO! My teacher yelled at us all the dang day!"*

What the "Experts" Do NOT Need. As shown, the responses to the survey focused almost exclusively on social and emotional needs, as well as the need to be less stressed and less overwhelmed. Only 2% of students asked for more academics or harder academics:

- *"I wish I had more math."*
- *"I'd like school better if we did math every day, I like math a lot."*
- *"Make math a little bit challenging especially for the higher up kids."*

More research would be needed to come to a definitive conclusion about this lack of request for more academics. However, when one considers that children have a natural love for learning, it becomes a

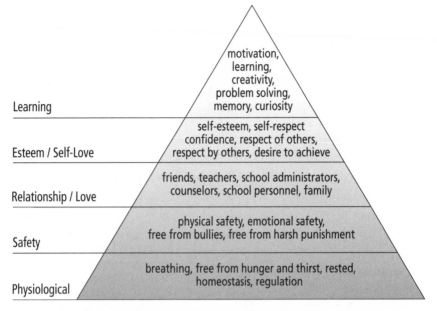

Figure 1.1. Hierarchy of learning.

likely conclusion that this natural desire is first dependent on meeting a child's social and emotional needs. The need to be calm and in balance, instead of stressed and overwhelmed, appears to be one of the student's top needs. The need to be safe, calm, understood, and accepted appears to take priority over education.

The students' survey responses fall directly in line with psychologist Abraham Maslow's hierarchy of needs theory. Maslow suggested that the needs of individuals must be met before they will have a strong desire for improving themselves and moving forward in their growth. In order of priority, Maslow theorized that individuals must have their physiological, safety, love/belonging/and esteem needs met prior to being motivated at the self-actualization level. He also believed that when these basic needs are deficient in one's life, the feelings of being anxious and tense are typically present.

Taking this framework of human motivation developed by Maslow, the same basic principles can be applied directly to the student in the classroom. Figure 1.1 shows how a hierarchy of learning pyramid can be used to create an understanding of a student's needs in the classroom. Instead of addressing the top of the pyramid, this book will address everything below the top in order to get to the top.

This single graphic in Figure 1.1 is a reflection of the entire contents of this book. To help the students addressed in this book, their physiological, safety, relationship/love, and esteem/self-love needs must be effectively addressed prior to any learning. This is where the change needs to happen in education—and it is a huge change. Yet it truly is the only way to help children who are struggling with their academic performance. We have, in the past, placed so much energy and focus on the top of the pyramid (with programs and academically focused solutions) that these students have behaviorally, socially, and emotionally collapsed, resulting in failing and out-of-control students.

It is up to us to find the courage to change our mindsets. It requires an entire paradigm shift. We must broaden the traditional "academics only" focus that has dominated our classrooms for far too long. Otherwise, the consequence is clear: We will continue to carry only a hammer and thus see every problem as a nail and continue to miserably fail our children.

There is another way.

Survey Says. The survey responses mentioned in this chapter are only a selection of the insights the students shared in the survey. Throughout Part Two of this book, other responses are given to reinforce the ideas discussed. Boxes like the one shown in Figure 1.2 will contain a response (exactly as

> ## SURVEY SAYS:
>
> ---
>
> "If teachers explained things better or differently."

Figure 1.2. Sample of how survey results will be presented throughout this book.

given from the participant) from the survey that directly relates to the adjacent section of text. Be sure to take note of each of these boxes, as they offer the answers needed to create a classroom environment in which children will excel to their full potential.

CHAPTER TWO

Regulation and Dysregulation

■

Feelings are not supposed to be logical. Dangerous is the man who has rationalized his emotions.

~ David Borenstein

"Waaaaa!" cries the baby in a vociferous protest, only to take a deep breath in order to begin again, louder and with more determination, "Waaaaaaaaa!"

Is this baby being rude and disrespectful because the parent is on an important phone call and cannot be interrupted? Of course not.

This baby is communicating that he* is in a state of stress; he is voicing his needs. He is unequipped to self-regulate, and he is unable to calm his own nervous system down. He does not have the ability to self-regulate and he is acting from an instinctual place to communicate his need for nurturing, food, or some other unmet need. In other words, this baby is unaware of anybody else's agenda. He cares nothing about his parent's important phone call; he refuses to be quiet even when his parent whispers "shhhhhh"; and he is demanding that his needs be met.

Does this sound familiar to how a student with difficult behaviors is often described in the classroom?

> *"Billy is selfish, disregards the classroom rules, interrupts the teacher when she is teaching an important lesson, refuses to stop talking even when reminded to settle down, disrupts the other children, and pays no attention to the feelings of his peers."*

Billy and the crying baby are more alike than what we have been able to realize in the past. Both children are "dysregulated" and both

* Throughout this book, the child is referred to as masculine in order to avoid clumsy construction.

children are acting in the only way they know how in order to return back to being "regulated." Each is seeking to find happiness and peace in this world but is grossly ill-equipped to know how to do this with polite manners. Each needs the help, guidance, and nurturing of a regulated adult to move back to a state of calm and peace.

Hyper- and Hypo-arousal. The crying of the baby and the behavior of Billy described above are examples of how children respond to stressful situations. These negative behaviors are natural human stress responses.

When children (as well as adults) become overly distressed, they react from a place of fight or flight. The fight response puts a child into a "hyper-aroused" state; conversely, the flight response puts a child into a "hypo-aroused" state. Definitions of these terms follow, and the corresponding behaviors for each are shown in Table 2.1.

Hyper-arousal is an increase in psychological and physiological tension, manifested by a reduction in pain tolerance, increased anxiety, exaggeration of startle responses, insomnia, panic, rage, and an accentuation of personality traits.

Hypo-arousal is the decrease in psychological and physiological tension marked by such effects as emotional indifference, flattened affect, irritability, low-grade nervousness, disengagement, depression, and hopelessness.

Table 2.1. Behaviors associated with hyper-arousal and hypo-arousal

Hyper-arousal	Hypo-arousal
Unable to focus or sit still	Defiant
Will not adhere to rules	Withdraws from peers
Aggressive	Tardy
Resistant to directives	Absent
Argumentative	Disassociates—shuts down
Anxious before tests	Avoids tasks
Impulsive	Numbs out—"I don't care" attitude
Risk-taking	Forgetful

The "Good" Child vs. the "Bad" Child. When a child is either hyper-aroused or hypo-aroused, he is "dysregulated." When a child is in a balanced state, in a state of homeostasis, he is "regulated." Some children, due to their early life experiences, live more chronically in a state of dysregulation than in a state of regulation. This is not a matter of choice or a matter of "good" child verses "bad" child; it is simply an imprint from their past histories.

To demonstrate these concepts, let me introduce two children we will be following throughout this book. These two children are based on children I have worked with clinically in the past. Their histories and stories are more real than what I could fictitiously create on my own. Please give a warm welcome to Andy and Billy:

Andy: As Andy was developing as a fetus, his mother was happy to be pregnant. She wanted to be a mother and adjusted her life to take care of herself during the pregnancy. She took her prenatal vitamins, ate well, and exercised. She decreased the stress in her life and had a supportive spouse who took care of and supported her. Andy reached full term and had a noneventful, easy delivery and was healthy when born. His mother breast-fed him, and both his mother and father cared for him around the clock. When he cried, he was soothed and nurtured. He stayed home for the first three years of his life under the care of one of either of his parents and never attended day care. He was gradually introduced to the school environment through short days at preschool and then moved to a small kindergarten environment by age five. When challenges happened in the home, as when his grandma passed, Andy was supported, given emotional space, and encouraged to express his feelings. By age eight, Andy was thriving in third grade and was an exemplary student.

Billy: As Billy was developing as a fetus, his mom was furious about being pregnant. Her boyfriend had lied to her about not being fertile. She tried to hide her pregnancy from her family but was discovered and kicked out of her home. She had no alternative but to go live with an abusive boyfriend. Billy was delivered four weeks premature, needed immediate medical attention, and was in an Isolette for the first two weeks of his life. Upon coming home from the hospital, his mother found a new job and placed him in day care at six weeks old. His mother had difficulty keeping employment and thus they moved frequently during the first five years of his life. He had multiple caregivers during this time. When his mother was home with him, she was quite unresponsive due to being overwhelmed, stressed, and without financial or emotional support. Billy had difficulty even in kindergarten, and by age eight his experiences in the school environment were more about being disciplined and punished than about learning and creating. He was the child the teachers dreaded having in class.

In a third-grade class, we have Andy and Billy, both eight years old and both adorable-looking little boys. Yet the contrast between these two children soon becomes painfully obvious to their teacher. Andy is able to pay attention, turns in his homework, follows the rules, plays well with his peers, and is helpful to the teacher.

Then there is Billy. Billy has a difficult time sitting still, fights the homework battle at home as if his life depends on it, is disruptive and loud in class, has social skills that are grossly immature, and fails to improve when given disciplinary action. This book is devoted to answering the ultimate and comparative question in order to find *Help for Billy*:

> **"Why are Andy and Billy, two children**
> **who appear to be so similar on the surface,**
> **so drastically different at every level?"**

One word is the answer to this question: trauma.

In the Beginning, There Was Trauma. No fancy EEGs, brain scans, or other specialized pediatric tests are needed to explain why Billy is different from Andy. Billy has experienced childhood trauma of the worst order; he has experienced trauma within the context of the parent-child relationship.

REGULATION AND DYSREGULATION | 11

Trauma is defined as any event that is more overwhelming than which is ordinarily expected. Such an event puts a child in the place of feeling out of control, scared, terrified, worthless, unlovable, insecure, and even endangered. When a child is belittled, degraded, ridiculed, threatened physically, threatened to be abandoned, withheld affection, withheld care and love, or neglected emotionally or physically, trauma has occurred. Less obvious and unrecognized traumatic events occur when a child feels as if his only value lies in meeting someone else's needs.

In Utero. When a woman is pregnant and she experiences stress, her body produces chemicals that become part of the growing fetus's makeup. Elevated levels of the stress hormones cortisol, epinephrine, and norepinephrine are released within the mother's body and have a negative influence over the fetus's ability to develop optimally. These stress hormones constrict blood vessels, resulting in a reduction of oxygen to the uterus.[1]

One study showed that children exposed to elevated levels of cortisol in the womb may have trouble paying attention or solving problems later in life.[2] Other studies continue to show that children born from stressful womb environments may be at greater risk for a variety of other stress-related pathologies and that the stress in the womb can affect a baby's neurobehavioral development.[3] If a fetus could talk to his mother, he would likely say, "Mom, you're stressing me out!"[4]

This stressful in utero experience marks the initial imprint of a child's ability to self-regulate. The effects of this nine-month experience can show up eight, ten, twelve years later for children like Billy—students who cannot sit still and are unable to pay attention in the classroom because their nervous systems were hardwired at an elevated level. It is not a case of "won't" but "can't" sit still.

Early Childhood Trauma. Children are vulnerable. In an optimal environment, they are not expected to experience this vulnerability until later in life when their minds and nervous systems are equipped to handle elevated levels of fear, stress, and overwhelm. Parents and caregivers are charged with the responsibility of creating environments of safety, security, and love for their children. Yet, the key phrase here is "optimal environment." Unfortunately, we live in the "real" world, so children will often find themselves in situations that are far beyond their window of stress tolerance. Trauma is prevalent in everyday life.

Not all trauma can be avoided, and there is not a child who emerges from childhood unscathed to some extent.

Childhood trauma happens at both the emotional and psychological level and it becomes defined by the child's perception of the event. Any situation or event that leaves a child feeling overwhelmed and alone needs to be considered trauma.

In general, a stressful event is likely to become a traumatic experience if:

- It happens unexpectedly.
- The child is unprepared for it.
- Someone has been intentionally cruel.
- The child feels trapped.
- The feeling of powerlessness prevails.

During the traumatic event, the impact is even greater if the child believes he is:

- Unlovable
- Worthless
- Forgotten or abandoned
- Powerless
- Helpless
- Hopeless

The last three—powerless, helpless, and hopeless—are the big three. When a child experiences one or all of the big three, he begins to believe the world is dangerous. Repeated experiences of these feelings will create, within this child, a lasting imprint from which he operates and behaves. A framework based in fear and survival becomes the child's viewpoint of the world around him. The more frightened and helpless a child believes he is, the deeper the fear imprint, the deeper the trauma.

Table 2.2 lists various possible childhood events that can be considered traumatic. These specific events, however, do not guarantee that the child will be traumatized simply because of the event itself. It is the perception and the emotional interpretation of the event that classifies it as trauma or not. It is about the feeling of being safe or not and it is always determined by the child's perspective—not reality.

Table 2.2. Events with the potentiality of childhood trauma

Possible Traumatic Childhood Events	
• Separation from a parent	• Single-parent households
• Disruptive home life	• Two-parent working households
• Medical procedures and/or serious illness	• Multiple siblings
	• Poor nutrition
• Unmet needs	• Foster care
• Mother with post-partum depression	• Adoption
	• Car accidents
• Poverty	• Deaths in the family
• Lack of a stimulating environment	• Parent's failure to express affection
• Racial discrimination	• Depressed parent
• Sexual, physical, or verbal abuse	• Absent parent
• Divorce	• Unattuned parent
• Neglect	• Overwhelmed parent
• Bullying (including from siblings)	• Witnessing community and televised violence
• Absence of consistent rules and boundaries	• Parent's failure to praise and encourage
• Parent's emotional rigidity	• Frequent moves
• Domestic fighting or violence	

While many of these types of events occur frequently in our society, such as divorce (which is the death of a family), the way a child perceives them should never be minimized or considered "normal."

Obviously, every child is going to experience some degree of trauma. Whether or not the trauma is going to have a lasting effect on the child depends on the how well the fundamental needs of physical safety, emotional connection, and predictability are met for the child. When children are given environments of support, love, and attention and when needs are met, the impact of traumatic experiences is minimized, and in many cases, avoided.

Bruce Perry, M.D., explains that "a confident, well-regulated adult can take a child out of a fire and have less trauma than an anxious dysregulated adult conveying fear to a child who falls off his bike."[5] *An event is not traumatic for a child based on the event itself; it is traumatic based on the response to the event from the caregiver.*

The Impact of Trauma. Hence, we have Andy and Billy and it is Billy for whom we need to find help. To understand both Andy and Billy, it takes understanding their histories, the nature of their relationships, and the environments in which they have lived.

Andy, when experiencing increased levels of stress (high arousal), was met with the care, love, and emotional and physical safety of his caregivers. He was calmed and thus quickly and easily returned back to a state of homeostasis and balance (calm arousal). Research shows that "the broader the range of emotions that a child experiences, the broader will be the emotional range of the self that develops."[6] By eight years old, Andy has confidence in himself and a regulatory system that is sufficient to function successfully in a classroom.

Billy, on the other hand, has not been as fortunate. He experienced chronic overarousal in utero. He was baked in cortisol before he even entered into human history. The disruptive lifestyle of his mother kept him living in a state of perpetual stress and fear, with little relief. He has an overabundance of high arousal experiences with a drastic shortage of calm arousal experiences. Billy only knows chaos and fear. This is his familiar. This is Billy's reality and this is *his* normal. Research continues to show that early and prolonged trauma in childhood affects an individual's ability and capacity to self-regulate.

To compare Billy to Andy or to expect Billy to act like Andy is not only unfair, it is judgmental. Unconditional love is about accepting someone perfectly, completely, and without a different expectation. Unconditional love requires us to accept Billy for exactly who he is. He cannot be different at this present moment. He is perfectly normal based on his history.

Billy's behavioral issues in the classroom are thus no longer behavioral issues. They are manifestations of trauma. They are stress-induced responses stemming from an insufficient regulatory system. His trauma has sensitized him to be either over-reactive or under-reactive (hyper- or hypo-aroused); there is no other option. This is his programming.

The challenge then presents itself to Billy's educators and caregivers as to how to help, guide, and teach him to calm his nervous system. He needs to be able to integrate his traumatic experiences in order to help him return to an internal state of peace and calm. His fundamental level of reactivity must be addressed first to equip him to be able to sit in the classroom and be an engaged and motivated student achieving academic success.

Internal Regulation. Internal regulation relates to the child's ability to regulate both physiologically and psychologically. From a physiological perspective, "the body bears the burden."[7] A child who has not had the experience of being settled, loved, and nurtured during times of heightened stress (as in the case of Billy), has an internal regulatory system that is not equipped to self-regulate.

When babies are born, they do not have an internal system equipped to self-regulate or self-soothe. When they cry, it is a cry for help to attract the attention of their caregiver to have their basic needs met. The biological design is for the caregiver to be the external regulator for the child since the child's internal system is underequipped. The infant is at the mercy of the caregiver to mold and develop its internal system of regulation. The infant is learning how to maintain a constant internal environment of homeostasis through this relationship.

When a child does not have his basic needs met from his caregiver, he does not learn how to respond or restore himself back to a calm state when stress-inducing events occur. The child has a limited ability to maintain a calm internal presence when the external environment presents challenges.

Neuroscience has shed light on the fact that the two-way interaction between a baby and its primary caregiver constantly adjusts and modulates the baby's exposure to environmental stimuli. This interaction serves as a regulator for the developing baby's internal sense of balance and homeostasis, creating an early childhood blueprint of peace and safety.[8] The regulatory role of the caregiver to the child is an essential ingredient to the normal development of the brain. In other words, relationship drives brain development (Figure 2.1).

John Bowlby, the "father of attachment theory," used the analogy of the thermostat to explain how a child is hardwired to depend upon the regulatory efforts of the caregiver. When a room becomes too warm, the thermostat sends a signal for the air conditioner to be activated. The air conditioner then turns on and re-regulates the comfort level of the room. Similarly, the baby is sending the signal that he is becoming dysregulated. He is trying to "activate" the parent. The baby needs the care, attention, nurturing, and calm presence of the parent in order to calm down his internal system ... he simply cannot do it on his own. The parent serves as the regulator and becomes the child's secure base.[9]

Figure 2.1. A healthy parent-child relationship drives healthy brain development.

The same is true for older children who did not receive these early childhood experiences of soothing. They missed these pacifying experiences and have not been taught through the context of the relationship *how* to calm down. Their internal stress systems are at a heightened level and, like Billy, by third grade (or even as far as middle school or high school) the new "normal" of their stress response system is far more elevated than their peers.

Their internal regulatory systems have been compromised and they are ill-equipped to handle stress, pain, or overwhelm. These children live in a perpetual state of internal dysregulation because they have never had a structure to assimilate and integrate stress. Hence, their behaviors are demonstrative of the internal chaotic world churning inside of them.

External Regulation. When the teacher says to Andy, "Andy, can you please settle down and quietly have a seat?" Andy has the internal regulatory ability to respond appropriately to his teacher. However, when Billy is asked the same question, his response is much different. He takes the long way around the classroom to his seat, he continues to not only talk but projects his voice across the room as if he is still out in the playground, and once seated continues to squirm and wiggle.

Traditionally, we have interpreted Billy as a disruptive child, pasted the label ADHD (attention deficit hyperactivity disorder) onto him, and reprimanded him for his "naughty" behavior. What we have failed to see is that Billy *cannot* settle down on his own. His internal system has not experienced the appropriate patterning to know how to be well behaved like his classmate Andy.

The brain-body system is a pattern-matching machine. A child with little internal self-control will pattern himself according to his past external experiences. If his past experiences have been chaotic, disruptive, and overwhelming, he will continue acting this way until new patterns are established. Thus, a child coming into a calm and safe classroom is still likely to be acting as if he is in his previous chaotic environment. A child can be taken out of trauma but not so easily can the trauma be taken out of the child. Past patterns of chaos are now the current framework for navigating his world; he knows no different.

The most effective way to change these patterns comes through safe, nurturing, attuned, and strong human connection. For the student in the classroom, it comes through the teacher-student relationship. The reality is, for Billy to learn and achieve academically, he must also be engaged at the relational level.

Environmental factors also play a significant role in providing a child external regulation. The ability to influence a child's internal system by external means has been demonstrated in scientific studies. In the 1970s, scientists reported that sound and musical rhythms could change a child's bodily processes. In Johannes Kneutgen's paper "On the Effects of Lullabies," he reported that the soothing effects of lullabies changed infants' breathing rhythms.[10] Other similar studies reported that heart rate changes were directly correlated to changes in the tempo of music.

Does this mean we should play lullabies in the classroom to settle children like Billy down? Perhaps, but what it essentially means is that we must take the responsibility to create environments for children that are designed to externally regulate them. A regulated environment can mean everything to a child who has a compromised internal regulatory system. Consider taking Billy and Andy to Chuck-E-Cheese's. What would be the difference between these two children in this type of setting?

Chuck-E-Cheese's is overwhelmingly stimulating with loud noises, lights blinking off and on, the promise of winning that special toy, and children running around with high energy. Andy would be able to have fun and could tolerate this level of external stimulation. Billy, on the other hand, would decompensate very quickly if left to his own internal devices.

The same holds true for a child like Billy in the classroom. Providing a classroom to support Billy's regulation is a responsibility that cannot be ignored or minimized. Failure to do so puts Billy at risk for cycling into a negative academic experience that can have lifelong consequences to reaching his full potential. (See Part Two of this book for more "when the rubber hits the road" ways to create a Beyond Consequences classroom for children.)

Window of Stress Tolerance. A child's window of stress tolerance is defined by his ability to withstand pressure, overwhelm, and fear without becoming dysregulated and without reaching his "breaking point." Each one of us has a certain level of stress from which we operate, as well as a point at which we reach complete overwhelm, where we essentially "blow."

Figure 2.2 shows the average level of stress both Andy and Billy typically live with—their internal baseline of stress when they start each day. We see that Andy's internal baseline of stress is low while Billy's internal baseline of stress is high.

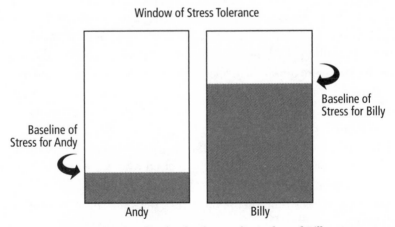

Figure 2.2. Baseline levels of stress for Andy and Billy.

Working Within the Window. The point from this baseline to a child's breaking point creates the "window of stress tolerance." Figure

2.3 shows the large window of stress tolerance for Andy and the small window of stress tolerance for Billy.

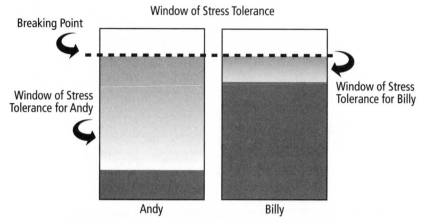

Figure 2.3. Window of stress tolerance for Andy and Billy.

When a child has a large window of stress tolerance, he has the ability to function well in life and at school. Working within the window, he has the ability to maintain himself in the classroom because he has more tolerance when stressed. In this state, his executive functions are intact and he is able to demonstrate the following:

- Self-control
- Short-term memory
- Emotional control
- Focus
- Task initiation
- Planning
- Organizing
- Time awareness
- Flexibility
- Moral judgment (knowing "right" from "wrong")
- Logical and sequential thinking (if "A" happens, then "B" will follow)
- Interpersonal skills (the ability to relate)

With this understanding, it makes sense why Andy can remember to bring his homework home, keep his backpack organized, show self-control when a classmate steals his pencil, and initiate a helping hand to his teacher. Andy has a much larger window, which gives him a large emotional range and emotional flexibility. He can navigate his way through his academic day with ease and flexibility.

Billy has a very small window. He lives only moments away from his breaking point. He is short on patience, is impulsive, has difficulty staying focused, and cannot comprehend why he cannot go to recess even after his teacher warned him three times earlier that if he did not behave he would miss his fun time. His executive functions are not on line because he is too stressed out to think clearly and rationally. He is living from a much deeper emotional place of internal chaos, fear, and survival. He has a much smaller emotional range, and struggles by expending a tremendous amount of energy to navigate his way through his academic day.

Changing the Window. When a child is placed in an environment that keeps him in his window without reaching his breaking point, he has a chance to increase his window. Being supported through an emotionally safe, nurturing, and calm relationship with his teacher allows his nervous system the chance to settle down. New neuropathways can be created and old behavioral programs that have kept him locked in a pattern of acting out can be rewritten.

Neuroscience is showing that the neuroplasticity of the nervous system can provide the answers for change and healing. "Plasticity" refers to the body's ability to add and remove connections, even into adulthood. Childhood is when the brain is the most plastic. Profound changes and healing can occur when a child is placed in the right environment; when his needs are met; when the relationships in his life offer acceptance, trust, and understanding; and when he is given the chance to have positive repetitious experiences in order to override past negative repetitious experiences.

The series of graphs in Figure 2.4 illustrate the level of healing that is possible for a student like Billy. Each positive experience allows for Billy's window of stress tolerance to increase, each time allowing new neuropathways to develop and new connections to be entrenched. While the healing process is not always as linear as depicted, over a period of time (sometimes as short as two weeks and certainly by six months) Billy's ability to handle stress will be noticeably improved.

Unfortunately, for many students their window decreases over the school year, instead of increases. The stress of the school environment builds throughout the year, especially during the weeks around state testing; these tests determine whether or not the child is promoted to the next grade.

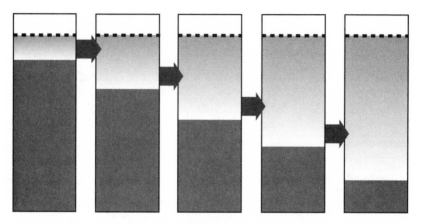

Figure 2.4. Increasing Billy's window of stress tolerance.

Even students like Andy, who start the school year with a large window of stress tolerance, often show signs of their window decreasing and of getting closer to their breaking point. The amount of pressure students are asked to handle in academic environments frequently goes far beyond what their nervous systems are equipped to handle. Staying at this heightened level of stress diminishes their abilities to self-regulate and their abilities to learn.

Traditionally, we have failed to realize that limited learning will happen if the emotional needs of a child are not met first. The hierarchy of learning, as shown in chapter 1, has not traditionally been acknowledged. A child like Billy cannot learn when he is living at the edge of survival—at the edge of his breaking point. Trauma alters to what the brain pays attention, so all of Billy's resources are dedicated to safety rather than academic achievement.

Instead of asking children to make a better "choice" in their behaviors, it is time that we ask ourselves to make a better choice in the creation of their environments. We must develop stronger relationships that will increase their window of stress tolerance and hence increase their capacity to learn, thrive, and succeed.

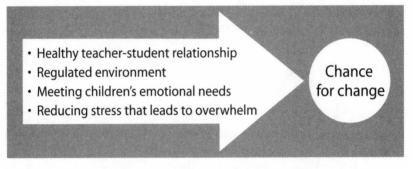

- Healthy teacher-student relationship
- Regulated environment
- Meeting children's emotional needs
- Reducing stress that leads to overwhelm

Chance for change

Figure 2.5. The necessary elements for change.

CHAPTER THREE

Anatomy of Learning

■

I felt a funeral in my brain.
~ Emily Dickinson

The 1990s were designated by Congress as the "Decade of the Brain." Yet more than a full decade after this era of discovery in brain research, our schools look remarkably similar to the schools of the 1950s.

Neuroscience has given us vast amounts of new understanding as to the plasticity and rewiring capacity of our neuronal circuitry. Neuroimaging technology has allowed us to see what areas of the brain are activated during times of rest versus times of arousal and fear. Additionally, we have learned that the human brain is exceptionally sensitive to social stimuli. However, neither of these history-making advances have changed the way we approach disruptive children in the classroom.

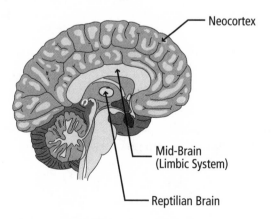

Figure 3.1. The triune brain.

Billy needs us to understand his brain because he deserves an effective education just as much as Andy. And the brain is vital to being able to help Billy because the brain is part of the process of change.

The Brain. There are basically three parts to the human brain: the neocortex, limbic system, and reptilian brain (Figure 3.1). While these three parts work together, each part has its distinct responsibilities and level of complexity.

Neocortex. The neocortex, also known as the rational brain, is the outer layer of the brain, and it distinguishes humans from other animals in the animal kingdom. It is the largest area of the brain, taking up about two thirds of the total brain mass. It is involved in the higher functions of human existence such as spatial reasoning, conscious thought, self-awareness, imagination, logic, planning, reasoning, higher-order thinking, language, and abstract thought. It is the center for foresight, hindsight, and insight. It is also involved in executive control, delayed gratification, and long-term planning, all-important characteristics of a "good" student in the classroom. This is the part of the brain where morals and ethics reside along with decision-making judgments between right and wrong. The neocortex is flexible, malleable, and has the capacity for infinite learning.

Limbic System. Paul MacLean, M.D., first coined the name "limbic system." This part of the brain includes the amygdala, hypothalamus, and hippocampus. The structure of the limbic system regulates mood, memory, attention, and hormone control. It is the main emotional center of the brain, the hub for what we feel and what feels good to us. It is the pleasure-seeking part of the brain. It records memories of behaviors and experiences that produce agreeable and disagreeable experiences. The limbic system is also concerned with self-preservation, fear, and the protective responses related to defense such as fight or flight. Emotions relating to attachment and relationship reside in the limbic system. This area of the brain handles the next fifteen seconds of life and gives us moment-to-moment survival.

Reptilian Brain. The oldest and most primitive part of the brain is the reptilian brain. This part of the brain includes the brain stem and the cerebellum. Vital life functions, like heart rate, digestion, body temperature, balance, circulation, breathing, stress responses, social dominance, and reproduction, are controlled in this lower area of the brain. The reptilian brain is concerned primarily with self-preservation, thus it is rigid, resistant to change, and obsessive.

As in the limbic system, life happens in this part of the brain in the next fifteen seconds, but even more intensely. There is no future. There is no tomorrow. There is no next week. It is believed that mental health issues such as obsessive compulsive disorder, post-traumatic stress disorder, and panic disorder have their roots in this area of the brain. This part of the brain is ready to respond at all times of the day, even in deep sleep.

Who's in Charge? Normally, the neocortex is in charge, keeping the limbic system and the reptilian brain in check. It exerts a top-down control over the survival impulses of the lower two parts of the brain (Figure 3.2). This is what gives us the capacity to live together in communities and to relate to one another in a kind, compassionate, and understanding way.

Top-Down Control

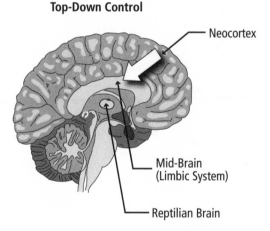

Figure 3.2. The regulated brain operates with a "top-down control" system.

We may feel impulses of anger and frustration from the limbic system, but when the neocortex is "in charge," we make decisions such as talking to someone rationally or letting it go and taking the higher road. If we are driving down the highway and someone pulls out in front of us, we may have thoughts of yelling at them or flicking them the finger, but instead of breaking into a rage of anger, we are able to squash these thoughts based on what is right and how our morals and ethics guide us. We are able to think of the consequences of our actions in the future so we can make a decision that is best for all those involved, not just ourselves.

However, when a child is in survival, this top-down control fails and the limbic system becomes more powerful in guiding behavior than the neocortex. At this point, it is not about morals, personality, or choice. It is at the level of instinct, emotionality, and survival.

This is an extremely important concept to understand because it explains why traditional behavioral techniques such as point charts and detentions do not work with Billy. When Billy is working from a bottom-up control system, what is "right" and "wrong" have no bearing on Billy's behavior (Figure 3.3). When Billy feels the impulse, desire, or need in the moment, he will make it happen for himself, despite the consequences of the future.

Bottom-Up Control

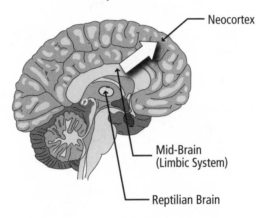

Neocortex

Mid-Brain
(Limbic System)

Reptilian Brain

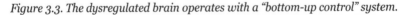

Figure 3.3. The dysregulated brain operates with a "bottom-up control" system.

Consequences do not register in the limbic system or reptilian brain. Remember, life happens in the next fifteen seconds here. The threat of having detention at the end of the day has no impact because in this framework of thinking, the end of the day does not and will never exist. Stickers have no influence. In fact, Billy might be more inclined to rip up the stickers rather than put them on a chart that is meaningless to him.

We can easily relate to this in our own experiences. The last time you made the commitment to eat healthy and lose weight, what happened when you got hungry and stressed? Chances are you did not grab the Brussels sprouts. You found chocolate and you ate it, and a lot of it, even though you made the commitment not to and you knew better. You knew the chocolate was counter to your commitment, but the consequence—gaining weight—was ignored in that moment when all you could think about was eating chocolate. Nothing else mattered. You wanted the chocolate so you ate the chocolate! You were in the pleasure-seeking "feel good" part of your brain and your neocortex was shut down, unable to control you from making the right decision. We have moments like this periodically, but the difference is that Billy has moments like this chronically.

The solution resides in settling Billy's system back down from a heightened fear and stress state to a calm and balanced state. Instead of addressing Billy's behavior with fear-based techniques or logically based techniques that do not register in his limbic system, the focus becomes addressing Billy's ability to regulate back to a calm state. Part Two of this book explains in detail ways to create a classroom environment that attends to Billy's need to return back to a top-down control.

"Every so often, he breaks into interpretive dance so his right brain doesn't atrophy."

Figure 3.4. Cartoon by Scott Masear. Reprinted with permission of CartoonStock (www.CartoonStock.com).

Left and Right Hemispheres. The neocortex is divided into left and right hemispheres. Each hemisphere has its responsibilities that are uniquely its own. The two hemispheres think differently, care about different things, and prioritize differently.

The left hemisphere is our conscious processor; the right hemisphere is our subconscious processor and has distinctly opposite functions from the left hemisphere, as shown in Table 3.1.

Table 3.1. Functions of the left and right hemispheres of the brain

Left Hemisphere	Right Hemisphere
Language	Nonverbal—pictures and imagery
Analytical thought	Intuition and imagination
Logic and reasoning	Random processing
Mathematics and calculations	Spatial abilities
Objectivity	Subjectivity
Cause-and-effect thinking	Reactive to all stimuli
Ego functions and consciousness	Face recognition and attachment oriented
Linear thinking	
Science	Symbolic thinking
Reality focused	Music and art
	Fantasy thinking

The differences between the two hemispheres will affect how children in the classroom learn. Numerous studies show the importance of teaching according to a child's dominant hemisphere. Educators and parents should take into consideration these findings for all students, our Andys and our Billys.

To help Billy in the classroom with his behavior, it is vitally important to take into account another distinguishing feature between the left and right hemispheres. Research has shown that the emotion of fear is processed in the right hemisphere, at the subconscious level, and trauma is all about fear. For Billy, when experiences in his past have not been processed and understood, the memory of these emotional and traumatic experiences resides at the subconscious level, without awareness.

The right hemisphere is essentially the brain's "red phone,"[1] whereby it acts in self-protective ways when challenged by overwhelm, stress, and pain. When memories are triggered by associational connections (present events and feelings that connect to past events and feelings), the right hemisphere dominates in its ability to act in the here and now. Only afterward is the left hemisphere then activated in a slower, more methodical and analytical manner.

The right hemisphere has a direct connection to the body, as seen in Figure 3.5. In other words, Billy does not have a chance to "behave." His system is hardwired to react and go into a self-protective bodily response. It may appear to be "bad behavior" to the untrained eye, but in reality it is simply Billy's normal response according to the programming of his body.

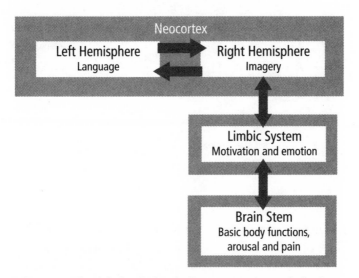

Figure 3.5 .The right hemisphere's direct connection to the brain stem.

Billy's Issues Are Not Behavioral; They Are Regulatory.
Working with Billy at the level of regulation and relationship addresses more deeply critical forces within Billy that operate at implicit levels, beyond the exchanges of language, choices, stars, and sticker charts. Traditional disciplinary techniques focus on altering

the left hemisphere through language and cognitive thinking. These traditional approaches are ineffective with Billy because his issues are not in this area of the brain. The problem is in the limbic system. Therefore, we must work to regulate Billy at the level of the limbic system in order to help him at the levels of language and cognitive thinking. See Figure 3.6 for a visual description of this concept.

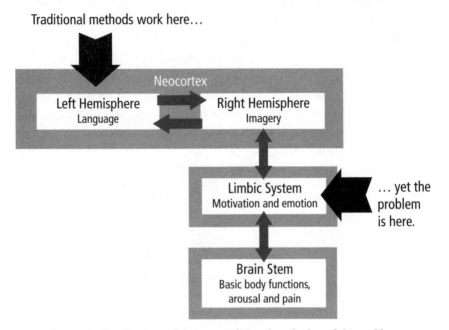

Figure 3.6. The disconnect between traditional methods and the problem.

The brain is growing at a rapid pace the first two years of life. An estimated 40,000 new synapses are formed every second in the infant's brain.[2] This growth and maturation is experience dependent on the social interactions from right brain to right brain between the caregiver and the child. The right brain is dominant for all children during the first two years of life to fully receive and interact with these nonverbal (visual, tactile) and verbal communications from the caregiver.[3]

Research suggests that the regulatory interactions between the child and caregiver during these primal years is essential for the brain's synaptic connections to develop normally and for functional brain circuits to be established. The attachment relationship is a major organizer for the brain during these primary years due to its ability to help the infant regulate emotions and states of stress.

Relationships that offer emotional availability from the caregiver give the child a chance to develop healthy and responsive regulatory systems. An emotionally available caregiver provides a dyadic interaction that is socially stimulating and rewarding. This attachment communication is dynamic, multisensory (auditory, verbal, tactile, and visual, including facial expressions), and reciprocal.

Relationship-based interactions continue to be a driving factor in a child's development well beyond the primary years. The engaging and safe social interactions in infancy provide the foundation and backdrop needed to later communicate with, understand, and successfully read future caregivers. The child's interpersonal neurobiology continues to crave connection and relationship throughout childhood in order to ensure healthy development into adulthood. However, when much of a student's early life experiences have activated the child's fear response system, the child develops a negative and hopeless blueprint rather than a positive blueprint organized by affection and optimism. Dominant experiences of fear, loss, abandonment, terror, distress, rage, and indifference from the caregiver create ill-formed neurological pathways. Overwhelming amounts of stress in childhood create a student who is limited in his window of stress tolerance and ability to modulate emotional and affective states.

As mentioned previously, children are resilient and plastic, meaning a child's nervous system and neurological pathways have plasticity: the ability to change, adapt, acquire, and create new and improved neurological pathways. It is in the relationship and emotional states of fear and overwhelm that the damage happens, so it stands to reason that it is in the relationship and emotional states of safety and love that repair and healing happen.

Interactive repair, or simply a safe relationship, is what it takes. The most important and most effective "behavioral technique" Billy needs in order to move him back within the behavioral boundaries of the classroom is relationship. Too much emphasis has been placed on what behavioral techniques should be used or which punishments should be imposed. Individual educational programs (IEPs) are fraught with techniques that are far removed from human relational experiences and they continue to fail to help Billy over and over again.

Typically, when a technique is used and it works, the credit has been given to the technique itself. Upon closer inspection, however, the question needs to be asked, "Was it the technique or the relationship that was the influencing factor?" Based on all the information presented to this point, the credit should not be given to the technique. Rather, it is the relationship that is at the heart of the child's experience. Techniques are merely layered on top of the relationship (Figure 3.7). It is the relationship—right brain to right brain—that is actually the driving force behind the change and helping children to get back on course.

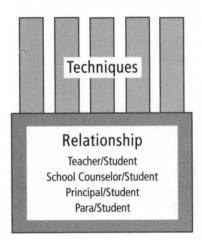

Figure 3.7. Relationship is the foundation to the effectiveness of techniques.

The Body. This chapter would not be complete without mentioning how the body holds the key to understanding Billy's ability to learn. The body is a powerful force in driving a child's behavior. Like all animals in the animal kingdom, humans go through a fight-or-flight response when danger is perceived. Because of Billy's perception of being threatened, even in what would normally be considered a safe school situation, Billy's bodily response will typically be in the range of survival.

While this response originates in the limbic system, it is the body that follows the "orders from headquarters." The limbic system releases hormones that prepare the body to take defensive action. The adrenal glands release epinephrine and norepinephrine to mobilize the body for fight or flight. The heart rate increases, allowing for more oxygen, and sends more blood into the muscles for quick movement. All systems are on alert and ready to protect. In this state, the limbic system will make a quick determination as to either fight or flee. If it is determined that there is adequate strength, time, and positioning for flight, then Billy will run and make an exit. Conversely, if it is determined there is not enough time or space to flee yet there is adequate strength to defend, Billy will fight.

There is also a third response, not yet mentioned, available to the limbic system: the freeze response, the least understood or appreciated response. If the limbic system determines there is a lack of time, strength, and positioning and death is in the realm of possibilities, the body will freeze. While this is a state of complete helplessness, it is also a state designed to lessen the pain from the attack of the predator by dissociating from the body and increasing the release of endorphins. It is a valuable state of survival because it decreases the chances of death. If the body becomes limp and lifeless, the predator (who responds to the movement of the prey) will most likely lose interest (as when a cat will no longer attack a lifeless mouse) and leave the prey alone.

The most important point regarding these three responses is that they are all automatic responses; they are not determined by mindful considerations at the level of the neocortex. It is not about Billy "making a better choice" or "choosing to do something different." Excitatory neurotransmitters and hormones are fueling these negative behavioral responses. The solution is not to ignite more of these responses by implementing a consequence, which will only be perceived as more of a threat by Billy. The solution lies in calming the brain in order to move back to a state of calm and safety at the body level.

The following story is adapted from real events reported in a local newspaper article.[4] It clearly demonstrates the activation and oscillation between the fight-or-flight survival response system for an elementary school student.

Eight-Year-Old Boy Arrested After Violent Attacks

Tuesday, an eight-year-old student was handcuffed at his elementary school. Officials said he attacked his teacher, a principal, and a police officer.

Reports indicate that the student became upset when his teacher told him he would not be going outside to the playground for recess with his classmates. The report made no mention as to the reason the student was being given this consequence.

The student became angry and tried to run out of his classroom. His teacher stopped him and said it was at that point the student began throwing chairs and overturning desks.

The teacher then called for help and when school personnel came in to control the student, he began head-butting his teacher and kicking the principal. He was escalating in his violence and was threatening to bite.

Police were called and when they arrived, the student attempted to escape by opening a window. The police officer pulled the student back in, only to be kicked in the head.

These efforts failed to calm the student down. Police officials did not disclose if the student had any documented condition that would have contributed to this incident.

Reports indicate the student is around four feet tall and weighs between seventy-five and eighty pounds. He was charged with disorderly conduct and assault and battery.

Here we have "Billy" who went from an angry state to being arrested and escorted out of his school by the police. By breaking down the chain of events that transpired, (see Table 3.2), it can clearly be seen how the interactions between the student and teachers, staff, and police contributed to this escalation.

Table 3.2. *Explanation of eight-year-old's behavioral responses*

Chain of Events in the Article	Explanation
Reports indicate that the student became upset when his teacher told him he would not be going outside to the playground for recess with his classmates. The report made no mention as to the reason the student was being given this consequence.	Billy becomes upset over the consequence of not being allowed to go outside with the other children. This consequence is reasonable for the teacher to implement, yet it is also reasonable for Billy, at age eight, to be upset. Billy wants to "fit in" and wants to be "normal" compared to his classmates. This is developmentally appropriate. Billy, however, appears to have a history of trauma that sends him deep into a state of fear because of this consequence.
The student became angry and tried to run out of his classroom. His teacher stopped him and said it was at that point the student began throwing chairs and overturning desks.	In his agitated and angered state, Billy is operating from his limbic system and thus cannot comprehend the logic of "if you don't behave, you don't go out to recess." It is unlikely the teacher connects with Billy at an emotional level but rather explains the consequence in a logical and rational manner. Billy perceives the logical discussion from his teacher as a threat because he cannot understand what she is saying. He now determines the situation to be unsafe. His body reacts and within a millisecond he is mobilized and equipped physiologically to defend. He slips into flight mode and attempts to leave. When he is stopped, he follows the fight/flight sequence and switches into fight mode.
The teacher then called for help and when school personnel came in to control the student, he began head-butting his teacher and kicking the principal. He was escalating in his violence and was threatening to bite.	School personnel come into the room to control Billy instead of regulate Billy. Control is perceived as a threat from a child in survival mode. Billy now goes from operating from his limbic system, simply emotionally upset, to operating from his reptilian brain, ready to preserve his life. He becomes primal—kicking and threatening to bite. He is like an animal under attack, fueled by his neurotransmitters to fight as if his life depends on it.

Chain of Events in the Article	Explanation
Police were called and when they arrived, the student attempted to escape by opening a window. The police officer pulled the student back in, only to be kicked in the head.	From Billy's perspective, the level of threat has been elevated exponentially. He switches into flight mode and attempts to flee from the premises to ensure his survival. The officer, doing what is right for Billy's safety, pulls him back into the building. However, Billy's brain determines this physical touch to be threatening, not rescuing. Now that escape is no longer viable, he switches once again into fight mode. The thought of being arrested and "in trouble" with the law has absolutely no impact on Billy because he is operating from a bottom-up control system. The neocortex is inaccessible to process this logic and reasoning.
These efforts failed to calm the student down.	The question begs to be asked, "What was actually done to calm him down?" More than likely, the interactions did not address Billy's level of fear; rather, the interactions appeared behaviorally based, attempting to control Billy.
Police officials did not disclose if the student had any documented condition that would have contributed to this incident.	Trauma is rarely seen as a condition that contributes to an episode such as this, but it needs to be. Billy's behavioral responses are classic fight/flight responses, surely induced by a history of being hardwired for survival.

This entire episode could have been avoided in the very moment Billy was given the consequence for not being allowed to go out with the other students. What likely happened in that moment was that the teacher reminded Billy of why he was getting a consequence or why he would have to accept her decision as final. Instead, the teacher could have connected with Billy in his limbic brain. Using the power of her relationship with Billy, she could have connected with his fear of not being included with the other children and the fear of being a "bad" child. To provide *Help for Billy*, the conversation could have unfolded like this:

> Teacher: "Billy, this is going to be hard, but you're not going to be able to go out to recess today because of what happened earlier."
>
> Billy: "But that's not fair!"
>
> Teacher: "I know. This can't feel good for you."
>
> Billy: "But it wasn't my fault!"
>
> Teacher: "Why don't you and I sit here and talk more about this so I can understand your perspective better."

The teacher could then spend ten minutes with Billy one-on-one to help him have a voice and to feel connected and understood. This is a "time in" with the teacher, used to regulate Billy's system and help to move him back into a top-down control. The consequence still holds: Billy does not go to recess. Ten minutes is likely all it would take to keep him from moving all the way down into survival as seen in the actual event. Taking ten minutes can seem impossible for a teacher with so many demands, but the alternative is to not take these ten minutes but take the time and energy of more staff, the principal, and the police.

Additionally, giving Billy this emotionally attuned conversation is giving Billy the experience of what it feels like to be in a positive and connected relationship. The more he experiences these types of interactions, the more he becomes equipped to handle stress in the future on his own, thus the more Billy has the ability to learn and achieve academically.

CHAPTER FOUR

Developmental Deficits

■

*The path of development is a journey of discovery that is
clear only in retrospect, and it's rarely a straight line.*
~ Eileen Kennedy-Moore

In 2005, revenues for Baby Einstein interactive products reached
$400 million. With the promise of enhancing a child's physical,
social, emotional, and academic development, these products have
flown off the shelves with parents' determination to make certain their
child has an extra edge over the child next door. Products such as
these pale in comparison to how drastically a child's development is
influenced in the early stages of life in the womb and during early
childhood by the attachment relationship. The brain is undergoing
major structural development, and its maturation is experience
dependent through the interactions of the parent and the child, not
through the interactions of a video and the child.

Healthy development is directly correlated to the intimate and
attuned relationship a child has with his caregivers. There is an emotional
and neurochemical effect that stimulates and regulates the child's
developmental progression through these interactions. Hence, a thirty-
minute Baby Einstein DVD is far less effective for creating an intelligent
child than a nurturing and emotionally enriched environment for a child
that will permanently influence his growing brain and nervous system.

When this attachment relationship is not in place, the child's
development is typically compromised and chaotic. He can have gaps
in some areas yet be overdeveloped in others. Thus, the early years of
a child's life prior to him entering a classroom are directly related to
his ability to function in the classroom—they correlate to either
academic frustration or academic achievement.

The impact of early life experiences can be seen in six developmental areas: (1) cognitive, (2) language, (3) academic, (4) social, (5) physical, and (6) emotional. The strength (or weakness) of these developmental areas will then influence the flow and ease of a child's learning and his ability to assimilate formal instruction. A gap in any one of these can result in challenges for the child, which typically show up as behavioral issues.

Many times Billy can sustain himself the first few years of school, but when he becomes more challenged academically, these developmental deficits rise to the surface. A student who once appeared to be on target and considered a "good" student can overnight turn into a "problem" student and become seriously behind in his level of achievement.

Most schools focus solely on academics. Students are expected to fit within an academic mold, regardless of whether their developmental journey has been erratic. This piece of their history is rarely recognized. The conventional academic environment works for a child like Andy. He fits the mold. Andy is developmentally on track in most, if not all, areas, as shown in Figure 4.1. He has only a few mild fluctuations.

The problem is that Billy does not fit this mold. His developmental path and ability to achieve normal milestones is erratic. He lacks the

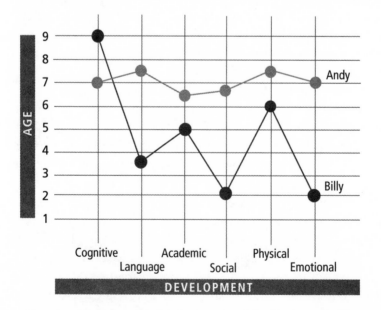

Figure 4.1. Comparison of Andy's development to Billy's development at age seven.

developmental skills and a strong emotionally secure foundation required to move forward with ease. Developmentally, he is all over the map. Figure 4.1 illustrates the chaotic development Billy brings to school every day due to his traumatic history.

Cognitive Development. The classic understanding of a child's cognitive development comes from the work of Jean Piaget. Piaget understood that children think differently than adults. He brought to the forefront the idea that children have to mature, or grow up, to understand the world around them fully. He believed that children cannot be expected to undertake certain tasks until they have reached a certain psychological maturity.

Piaget made the important point that children develop in stages and that the success of one stage is dependent on the mastery of the previous stage. In other words, a child has to complete the first level in order to move to the next level. If a thirteen-story building were to be built, the fifth floor could not be built until the four previous floors had been completed (Figure 4.2). Yet too many times, we expect Billy to start at the fifth floor when his first four floors are underdeveloped. He needs help getting a stronger foundation prior to moving forward in his development.

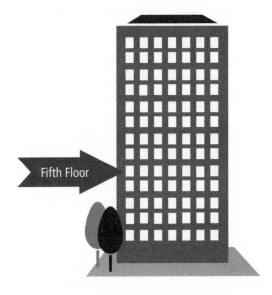

Figure 4.2. Progression of development is dependent on previous stages of development.

Cognitive development refers to the way a child perceives, thinks, and gains an understanding of the world. Cognitive skills give a child the ability to process the information he collects. These abilities include being able to analyze, evaluate, retain information, recall experiences, make comparisons, and determine the required action needed. Most cognitive skills are learned; when there is an interruption in this learning process for children, cognitive weaknesses result.

For many children like Billy, their cognitive development can be far more developed in some areas than the typical child of the same age. Teachers often express that their Billy is "more gifted than the gifted kids." Trauma can enhance "pockets" of a child's cognitive abilities because of the child's vigilance to learn about the world in order to protect himself. The philosophy of survival unfolds like this: "If I can develop a greater capacity to understand the world, I can then prevent more harm and pain, thereby keeping myself out of danger." Billy's brain becomes more capable of understanding, analyzing, and evaluating concepts than Andy's in certain areas. Ronald Federici, Psy.D., an internationally known neuropsychologist who specializes in evaluating children like Billy, calls these abilities "pockets of brilliance." These children may appear brilliant in certain areas, but in reality they are still lacking in some of the critical cognitive areas.

Because an increase in cognitive development may be driven by survival, the Billys of the world tend to be more concrete in their thinking. Live or die equates to black or white because black or white creates safety. There can be no gray areas in between because gray areas do not provide predictability, only uncertainty. Thus, the ability to think abstractly is compromised.

Billy tends to demand answers that are definitive, without being able to comprehend that more than one answer may exist. If there is only one answer, there is security. If there are multiple answers, there is less certainty and therefore Billy may also have the inability to see beyond the concept presented at face value. Ask Billy to read a paragraph and he can comprehend everything that was explicit in the reading. However, ask him to describe an implicit concept such as "What was the main idea in this paragraph?" and he will become confused and lost, appearing as if he was lying about even reading the paragraph.

Language Development. Language helps to form a child's thoughts and mental processes. Language development equips a child to organize, symbolize, and express himself to others.

Research has shown that language development begins prior to birth. The fetus becomes familiar in utero with the sounds and speech patterns of its mother's voice. This language learning then continues with one-on-one interactions between the child and his caregiver. These interactions not only develop the child's ability to speak the language, but they also develop and expand his understanding of the complexities of language and of people.

Social interactions with parents and other adults who lovingly engage and respond to a child's questions and conversations are critical to the child's language development. Children need adults to take the time to listen, talk, read, sing, and play games with them. It is not solely the language acquisition of being able to differentiate a "dog" from a "cat" that determines the child's ability to communicate and process. It also comes through the experiences of communicating interactively at an engaged social level. Language development occurs within the context of safe, secure, and reciprocal relationships.

When comparing Andy and Billy, it may first appear as if they are equal in their language skills. They both recognize and identify objects. They both spell basic words. They both speak the same language at about the same level. However, Billy's ability to accurately comprehend and organize his world through language is different. Words can be confused with other words. Nebulous communication creates confusion and misinterpretation. Intended meanings behind words and phrases are lost. Words with multiple meanings are baffling and aggravating, as seen in the following scenario:

Once when working with a nine-year-old "Billy," we took a break and I was checking my email on my computer. He looked at me and asked what I was doing. I replied, "I'm working on my computer." He gave me a perplexed look, so I tried to understand his confusion by asking, "Haven't you ever worked on a computer?" Billy replied, "No." We both sat there for a few moments of bewilderment. I was baffled and silently thinking, "He's nine years old. Surely he has worked on a computer before!" Billy then said, "Well, I've played on a computer before." "Of course!" I thought. In his mind, adults "work" on computers and children "play" on computers. In his black-and-white world, "work" and "play" were two very distinct and unrelated activities.

Due to this deficit in his language development, Billy can easily misinterpret his teacher's instructions, become frustrated when trying to communicate, and miss major concepts at story time because of his lack of language acquisition. As he becomes unable to understand the world around him, Billy acts out in frustration. The teacher is unable to understand him, sees his behavior as defiance, and then reprimands him. Billy becomes more confused and disorganized in his thinking as this scenario unfolds day after day, because all along the way he has never really understood what he has done wrong.

The greatest fallout from having language deficits is that Billy derives from this scenario that he is bad, stupid, and less worthy—all because he did not really "get" what was going on in the classroom to start. All of this is the result of him missing critical language experiences early in life with his caregivers, none of which were his fault. Billy is simply a child who was not given what he needed early in life to be able to be Andy.

Academic Development. To be successful in the classroom, a child needs to have a strong foundation of academic skills. The academic skills and qualities of a "good student" include a positive attitude, self-discipline, good organizational skills, an ability to focus and concentrate, and the willingness to persevere through difficult problems.

As children spend time in the classroom, their academic skills typically improve. They learn how to study more efficiently, take better notes, and take tests better. By high school, children like Andy have had enough positive experiences in their academic careers that they are soon ready to move on to college.

Trauma impacts a child's ability to concentrate, organize, and process information. So by age sixteen, Billy may still be unable to keep his backpack organized, his note-taking skills are probably nonexistent, and he likely has no ability to plan out the timing of a four-week project. His level of frustration with school has been continually building since the second grade, and by now he hates learning and has no tolerance for doing work he believes is "busy work." At this point in his academic career, Billy is truly viewed as nothing short of a problem student in the classroom.

The real issue, however, is that he never received the additional help he needed to overcome his limitations. He was simply expected to be like Andy and expected to catch up on his own. Yet this expectation was outside of his capabilities. Recovery is still possible, though. Billy will need the help and assistance of a willing teacher or adult to help guide and support him. Working one-on-one with Billy, even at a later stage of his academic career, can move him to success, as the next example demonstrates:

> *An eighth-grade Billy was failing at his mainstream middle school. The issue was not his level of comprehension of the material itself; it was his lack of ability to organize the material. He was unable to keep his locker organized and keep track of the various assignments for his six classes. His parents switched him to a school that recognized this organizational challenge. At the beginning of the school year, the back-to-school materials list was explicit as to the number and color of folders, the number and color of indexing tabs, the number and color of highlighters, and more. The school was taking on the challenge through these organizational tools to teach its students how to organize to reduce the students' level of overwhelm. Billy also had a school counselor work with him several days a week one-on-one to help him keep his locker organized. This added support allowed Billy to reach his full academic potential that year and helped him learn how to break out of the frustrating and overwhelming cycle he was in when it came to organizing.*

Social Development. Social development refers to a child's ability to interact with other children and adults. It begins at birth as a way to survive. As mentioned, a baby is unequipped to provide for himself or protect himself and thus must rely solely on his ability to attract the attention of his caregivers. Within these early parent-child interactions, it is the parent who gives to and cares for the child. The child is unable to reciprocate. The process of the child learning to move past his own needs, connect more equally, and reciprocate with others is the journey of social development.

Once a child enters school, it is expected he will have the social skills needed to relate appropriately to his teachers and peers. For children like Billy, however, they may be delayed in this developmental category. Healthy early childhood relationships are paramount to a child's developing appropriate social skills.

Due to traumatic early childhood experiences, children like Billy may still be more like a toddler (and in some cases, the child's social development is so arrested he can be as socially demanding as an infant). The child's interactions are self-centered and socially inept. This description pertains not only to younger children but to many teenagers entering high school as well. Some older children were never given the appropriate guidance and experiences to move past the toddler stage. They have been locked into a negative loop and simply expected to change without the proper help; they are stuck. These children do not know how to:

- Make friends
- Show empathy toward others
- Wait patiently
- Communicate anger in a healthy way
- Resolve conflicts peacefully
- Follow rules
- Maintain appropriate personal space
- Respond kindly to someone who is hurt
- Enjoy the company of others
- Maintain eye contact
- Express themselves emotionally
- Correctly read nonverbal communication
- Tolerate ups and downs in relationships

The classroom is a socially demanding environment. For Billy, the classroom poses a significant challenge, as he is unequipped to navigate through the nuances of positive social interactions, which in turn affects his ability to behave appropriately and succeed academically.

For Andy, social skills come naturally. His early relationships provided him the experiences to move far past being egocentric and demanding of others. When he enters the classroom, he is kind, interactive, and inviting to others.

Teachers and peers want to connect with Andy. Such is not the case with Billy—he can actually repulse and repel people. It takes understanding this social ineptness to see it beyond simply poor behavior. If Billy's gaps are recognized and given appropriate support (such as working in a social skills group, being gently reminded in the classroom as to what an appropriate response would look like, and having his teacher model good social skills), Billy has a chance to fill in the gaps and catch up to his peers. Here is a true story from one mother whose "Billy" repeated a grade because of his social and emotional needs, not his academic needs:

Billy was adopted at four years old from a Russian orphanage. By the time he was in third grade, it was becoming painfully clear that he was falling very far behind his peers. He was not being included in the social groups, and his expressive language was immature. Academically he was about average, so he did not need to be held back for another year based on his academic accomplishments, though we had concerns of the social implications he would face from being held back. Children can be cruel and say things like, "What? Did you fail? Are you so stupid that you have to repeat third grade again?" However, we decided that the long-term gain of giving him a chance to catch up with his classmates socially and emotionally far outweighed the short-term loss of being made fun of at school. We actually asked Billy how he felt about going forward to fourth grade or repeating the third grade (with the same teacher to give him familiarity) and he chose staying back. He was painfully aware of the fact that he actually was not fitting in with his classmates and that he was a bit lost socially.

Today, Billy is a senior in high school. I believe having him repeat the third grade was one of the very best parenting decisions we ever made for him. He is excelling at school, has friends, and would not have been ready to graduate last year.

*Being a senior now gives him one more year to adequately
prepare him for moving to the next major developmental
step in his life. I know deep down had we not made this
decision of retaining him, the last nine academic years would
have been needlessly difficult and challenging for him. It is a
joy to see him love school, have friends, and be happy in his life.*

Physical Development. As a child develops physically, he
improves his fine and gross motor skills along with his sensory skills.
Motor skills require coordination between the brain and the muscles,
allowing the child to crawl, walk, run, write, and speak. Motor skills
take practice and repetition in a stimulating environment in order to
become automatic and develop to their optimal level.

Sensory skills such as hearing, vision, and touch are responsible
for a child receiving information from his environment. The motor
skills then give the child the ability to express the information received
from his sensory pathways. In severe cases, children deprived of
proper nutrition, stimulating care, and basic nurturing will become
arrested in their physical growth, known as failure to thrive.

A child like Billy may be years behind in his ability to manipulate
a pencil. His fine motor skills may be delayed; thus, his ability to
coordinate the brain with his hand during writing time in the classroom
will prove to be beyond his window of tolerance. His body may be
highly sensitive to noises, bright lights, and other sensory-provoking
elements in the environment. His body cannot properly filter out and
prioritize sensory information, so he gets flooded and overwhelmed
easily. Billy may be physically smaller than his peers, creating a fear
dynamic in both the classroom and playground because he feels more
vulnerable. All of these factors would ultimately manifest themselves
into negative and inappropriate behaviors if left unidentified and
unaddressed.

Emotional Development. Children are emotional beings. They
are programmed at birth to express their emotional states through
crying and other attention-seeking strategies. As they mature, their
learning edge is for them to improve and expand their abilities for
emotional communication. This process of emotional development
continues through adolescence and into adulthood.

A student's emotional maturity can be a critical factor in his ability to do well academically—emotional maturity matters. Research indicates that students who have progressed in their emotional development have a significantly greater chance of early school success, whereas students who are more emotionally constricted in their development face grave risks of early school difficulty.[1]

Andy enters the classroom with the ability to identify, express, and cope positively with his feelings. He was given "emotional space" from his caregivers when he had feelings and needed to process them. Through the context of his early relationships, he was allowed to feel and he was loved and supported through the spectrum of his emotions. He learned words for feelings and experienced safety around uncomfortable and unsettling feelings.

Andy's ability to express himself now gives him the ability to reciprocate and tolerate other people's negative feelings. When Andy is in the playground and another student comes and steals the ball from him, he feels angry but has the ability to work it out with the other student or to think clearly enough to go seek help from his teacher.

In contrast, Billy enters the classroom with negative internal messages instilled in him that have constricted his ability to have a strong sense of self and to be free to feel at the heart level. He believes:

- "You shouldn't feel that way."
- "You're just being a baby. It's no big deal."
- "When people are angry, you will get hurt."
- "It isn't safe to feel."
- "You don't show your feelings—you'll upset those around you."

When Billy has feelings, he suppresses and internalizes them. This buildup of unexpressed emotions keeps him in a state of anxiousness and hypersensitivity—he becomes a ticking time bomb. It is not a matter of "if" he will blow but "when." Typically, if he has reached his storage capacity of these unprocessed feelings, he will react and experience an outpouring of feelings, typically unrelated to the actual incident. It will be a "straw that broke the camel's back" type of incident.

Should a student come up and steal the ball from seven-year-old Billy, Billy becomes immediately outraged. He taps into a well of feelings that have been brewing and goes into fight mode. He slugs the student who stole the ball and proceeds to pounce on him. This over-reactive response is not just about the ball; it is an outpouring of the depth of feelings that were locked down from earlier experiences. A moment of emotional release has arrived and Billy has little self-control or self-awareness to keep it in check. At age seven, Billy has the emotional maturity of a two-year-old. Chaos breaks out on the playground, and who is seen as the "bad" child once again? Billy.

A mother's recounting of how her "Billy" was constantly on the edge emotionally and was as emotionally insecure as an infant follows:

At the end of summer break, right before the start of third grade, I had a meeting with Billy's IEP team to come up with a plan to help him ease back into the school year (since he barely made it through the second grade). We decided that every day I would come have lunch with him, stay for recess, and then help him transition back to class. Since I drove him to school, walked him to class, and also picked him up from school, this meant we would not go for more than three hours without connecting.

But one day I was on a business call at home and completely lost track of time. I realized I was going to be twenty minutes late so I flew down the stairs, jumped in the car, and frantically tried to reach his teacher by phone the entire drive there, all to no avail. I rushed to the cafeteria but nobody was there. I headed to the playground and before I could make it to the door, three staff members burst through it carrying Billy screaming, crying, and kicking. The teachers said he got into a fight with a boy outside over a jump rope and could not be calmed down. One of them started asking him about the fight but this only elevated Billy's reactivity. I got down on the floor where he was still crying and apologized for being late. He looked at me and said, "Why didn't you call me? I thought you were dead!" It was never about the jump rope.

The update to this story is that Billy is now eleven years old and is in the sixth grade. While he still attends a school for children with special needs, he is able to be at the school the entire day for five days a week on his own. His mother no longer has to break his days into small chunks of time without her presence. He is growing, maturing, and healing emotionally and is much closer to being able to sustain himself independently.

CHAPTER FIVE

Belief Systems

■

Whether you think you can, or
you think you can't—you're right.
~ Henry Ford

"**I** am the greatest."

At a very early age, Muhammad Ali began saying these words with confidence, conviction, and emotion. He bragged and told everyone these words even before he proved he was the greatest.

And indeed, Muhammad Ali did become the greatest. In his professional boxing career, he had a record of fifty-six wins, five losses, and zero draws. He was unstoppable and impenetrable.

How did he manifest these words into reality? He told himself he was the greatest, and he told the world he was. Muhammad Ali became his belief, he trusted his belief, and thus, his belief became his reality. His belief system was the single most important influence he had over his life. From this poignant example, it can also be said that one of the most important influences over a child's level of academic success is his belief system.

Our belief systems are at the core of who we are. They drive us. They persuade how we act and on what we put our attention. A belief is this powerful because it is simply any perception, cognition, emotion, or memory that we consciously or unconsciously assume to be true. In short, our belief is our reality.

Beliefs can be empowering and life changing, as in the example of Muhammad Ali, but unfortunately they can also be equally as disempowering. If our beliefs are negative, pessimistic, and limiting, then the result will be a negative, pessimistic, and limiting existence. For Billy, this destructive power of a negative belief system is what creates much of the chaos in his academic experience.

The Origins of Our Beliefs. Children come into this world with a natural propensity to completely trust, as fact, what others say to them. As children grow, mature, and as their brains develop, their ability to receive, filter, and delineate beliefs also grows. The neocortex does not fully develop until a person is twenty-five years of age, in an optimal environment. As Jean Piaget emphasized, children are not little adults. The brain is different at each developmental stage of their lives.

Conception to Birth. Belief systems begin in the womb and are highly influenced by the mother, the first human connection of the fetus. The developing fetus is highly sensitive to its mother's feelings during the pregnancy. If the pregnancy is unplanned and the mother does not want to be pregnant, these feelings will transfer to the fetus. He will feel as if he is unwanted and unlovable. This becomes part of his cellular system as the child's genetics are still spinning and forming. If the mother is under stress and unhappy, the fetus begins to absorb this and formulates the belief that he is the cause of this unhappiness. The foundation of the baby's "lovability" and self-worth is encoded into the cells of his body these first nine months.

Birth to Two Years Old. At birth, the biological design is for the child to be connected to his mother. Mother and child are a dyad—a system of two that has become one. The infant is vulnerable and is completely relying on the mother for all that exists.

In this connected and entwined relationship, all that is the mother's belief becomes the child's belief, as it did in the womb. If the mother believes her child is a burden and an inconvenience, the child too believes he is a burden and an inconvenience. If the mother believes the world is unsafe and dangerous, this too becomes the child's belief. The accumulation of these rejecting and unsafe feelings from the mother eventually turns into a deep-seated state of self-rejection. Hence, we have a child like Billy.

Conversely, if the mother loves herself, is happy and optimistic, the child too loves himself and is happy (barring any other factors that would interfere with this transfer of belief systems, such as a physical condition that causes continual pain). If the mother finds meaning in being a mother, so too does the child find meaning and purpose in this world. These loving and accepting feelings from the mother turn into self-acceptance and self-love. Hence, we have a child like Andy.

Two Years Old to Ten Years Old. As a child begins to mature and the brain develops, a child begins to develop his own identity, his own programs, and his own beliefs. These programs and beliefs, however, are based solely on his life experiences, what is said to him, and what he experiences in the context of relationship.

At this point in development, the brain is still only a receiver. It is an open mind, soaking in all information as truth. The brain at this stage of life does not have the capacity to process or filter out the negative. It internalizes everything.

If a child is told negative messages, these then become part of his conscious and subconscious belief system of who he is. If he is told, "I wish you had never been born," there is no ability to block this statement from becoming part of his reality. He then believes unequivocally that he is not loved or worthy.

Children at this age observe the behavioral patterns of those closest to them. They learn to distinguish acceptable and unacceptable social patterns according to their immediate environment. These perceptions have been downloaded into the child before age six, and they shape and influence how the child will interact with others from this point forward.[1]

Unfortunately, by the time a child is eight years old, he is typically told seven times more negative messages than positive messages. What is said to children at this vulnerable age does matter, as do the experiences the child has with the adults in his life. It molds the very essence of who this child becomes and who he perceives himself to be in this world. Neuroscientist Andrew Newberg, M.D., author of *Why We Believe What We Believe,* clearly points out that the expression "Monkey see, monkey do" turns out to be neurologically correct.[2]

Ten Years Old to Sixteen Years Old. As a child moves into preadolescence and the teenage years, the brain becomes more sophisticated. Instead of being strictly a receiver, it also becomes a processor. The child now has the ability to begin to filter out programs that do not work for him and that are not his truth. He becomes aware that he is a separate and unique individual with the power to create his own beliefs.

During this time, the brain becomes sophisticated enough to understand and comprehend that many of the things that were said to him or what happened to him were not good and not right. This stage in a child's development is a time for self-reflection and for filtering out invalid beliefs. However, this is a new process with a steep learning curve. Instead of being able to discern the nuances of the true and false beliefs, the child becomes extreme. He filters out everything from adults simply because they came from adults. This manifests into the typical teenager who is rebellious, disrespectful, and defensive in his behaviors and attitudes.

While the child is simply trying to reject negative beliefs that were taken in as truths, the process of cleansing becomes black and white, all or nothing. Statements like "You're not in charge of me!" or "I don't have to listen to anything you say" are all too familiar to anyone working with teenagers. Such statements are reflective of the very charged process of self-identity and the refining of the individual's own belief system.

External Messages Become Internal Realities. Children's beliefs are created when experiences happen over and over again and when phrases are spoken repeatedly. Beliefs get stronger when more evidence supports them. The mind is like the software of the brain. A child's mind is "programmed" by his experiences, and this becomes the "software" by which he perceives and operates in the world.

A child is not born into this world knowing he is worthy, loved, or all right. It is by the design of the parent-child relationship that these beliefs are to be "installed." Whether or not these beliefs are positive or negative is irrelevant. All beliefs become real because the child has no filters to discern true beliefs from false beliefs. They become a tremendous power and driving force in the child's life.

This can easily be seen in the biomedical literature. The placebo effect shows us that when a physician believes in a treatment and the patient has faith in the physician, the outcome, despite a true intervention, is improvement and sometimes a complete cure in the patient's condition.

What we say to our children and how we interact with them does matter. Their brains use these messages to develop their sense of self as well as to make sense of their worlds. When children are given a message, any message, they translate it into meaning.

The mind will take a statement, create an interpretation of the world from this statement, and create a deeper meaning from this statement. For instance, if someone says, "Have a safe flight," there must be a reason for this statement. The reason, based solely on the words used, must mean that flying is unsafe. If flying were safe, then there would be no need to voice a hope for safety. The only conclusion is that there must be some sort of risk associated with flying.

Apply this same concept to typical messages we give to children. Table 5.1 shows what message we are saying to them and their concrete and linear interpretation of the message.

Table 5.1. Examples of how external messages lead to negative internal beliefs

External Message	Internal Belief
"Play safely."	Play must be dangerous.
"You can try harder."	My best isn't good enough.
"You should have studied more."	I'm not good enough.
"If you would just listen."	I'm stupid.
"Why can't you be more like the other children in this classroom?"	I don't fit in.
"You are old enough to do this on your own."	I'm alone.
"How many times do I have to tell you not to do that?"	I can't change, so it isn't even worth the effort.
"I'll write you up."	It is me against you. I need to fight you.
"From someone with your record, that doesn't surprise me."	People don't believe in me; therefore, I don't believe in myself.
"I'm going to have to use some 'tough love.'"	Love is dangerous.
"You're making me angry."	I am bad.

Beliefs Influence Physiology. Studies show that those with optimistic viewpoints and belief systems who say "everything will work out" have stronger immune systems. Additionally, optimistic people's secretion level of cortisol (a stress hormone) is less.[3] Therefore, beliefs affect physiology and have influence over the emotional center of the child's brain. Strong beliefs, both positive and negative, elicit strong emotions and thus arouse the limbic system of the brain.

If a child has strong negative beliefs, this will be associated with strong negative emotions, keeping the child in a state of stress and overwhelm, keeping the limbic system activated. If you have ever felt bad about something you did, even long after the event, the emotionality of the event lingered with you. You most likely felt anxious, tired, and simply "off" because of these feelings. For children like Billy, the same is true, but instead of a being in a temporary state of dysregulation, he remains in a perpetual physiologic state of dysregulation, greatly influenced by his belief system.

Not only does the emotionality of the belief keep the belief system deeply ingrained into the child's internal framework of the mind, but the neural circuits are also being engraved to reflect these beliefs. The development of the neuropathways is being set according to these beliefs. Neuroscience is showing that the more that a particular neuronal path is used, the stronger it becomes. In other words, neurons that fire together wire together. Conversely, the less a particular neuronal path is used, the weaker it becomes. It is a case of "use it or lose it."

For example, if Billy's parental reactions to his behaviors growing up were constantly about failure and blame, his sense of value and self-worth will be diminished. He has been programmed to believe, "I'm not good enough" and "Nothing I do is right." His neural network is wired together in a negative, self-defeating pattern.

Conversely, if Andy's parental responses to his behaviors growing up reflected continuous understanding, support, and loving guidance, his sense of value and self-worth will be strong and unshakeable. He has been programmed to believe, "I can do it" and "I am good enough." His neural network is wired together in a positive, self-supporting pattern.

As Billy and Andy arrive in the classroom side by side, they are viewed as two similar students from their external appearances, but internally Billy and Andy are drastically different. They cannot be expected to each fit into the same academic mold and perform at the same academic standard without Billy receiving additional support in the beginning.

Beliefs in the Classroom. Once Billy enters the classroom, even though his belief system has already been negatively influenced, and in many cases corrupted, it is important to understand how the dynamics and protocols within the school environment can also negatively and positively influence Billy's belief system. Two of the most impactful for Billy are the grading system and the use of praise as encouragement.

Grading System. As early as kindergarten, children learn that a big red "X" on their worksheet means they are "wrong." Enough of these X's and the only viable conclusion becomes "I'm stupid." If Andy receives no X's and Billy receives five X's, when Billy compares his sheet to Andy's sheet, the only logical conclusion Billy has to make is "I'm dumb" and "Andy is smarter than I am." In contrast, if Andy receives all check marks, he believes he is smart but then he also begins to associate his worthiness with his performance.

The mind believes what it perceives as factual. Even if the teacher works to console Billy by telling him not to worry, Billy can only believe what is tangibly staring him in the face. The five X's are factual. The consoling words are only fictional.

The American grading system is set up to give children the message that they are either "smart" or "stupid." While this system is detrimental on its own merit, when a child like Billy enters the classroom already programmed to believe he is unworthy or stupid, this grading system can be disastrous. It reinforces negative beliefs and ultimately closes any door of opportunity for change. Learning can be stopped dead in its tracks at this point.

Praising as Encouragement. For a child like Andy, using praise as a form of encouragement is effective and well received. However, for a child like Billy, whose deep-seated belief system says he is no good and not worthy of praise, it can have a sabotaging effect.

Teachers become exceptionally frustrated when they give a child like Billy a compliment and only seconds later he acts out in the opposite direction. It is as if Billy had an agenda to prove he is truly a "bad" child. It can be maddening to witness this type of behavior.

Billy's world has been so unpredictable and unsafe that his stability is based on his beliefs. He has to believe what he believes to survive. Giving up these beliefs would be not only scary but terrifying. He has to work to prove to the world he is "bad"; hence, compliments and praise drive him to act out even more negatively.

Words like "Great job, Billy. I'm so proud of you!" blatantly contradict Billy's internal framework. Messages like these are in direct contradiction to his sense of self. Newberg writes, "The human brain has a propensity to reject any belief that is not in accord with one's own view."[4] Billy's entire foundation of existence can be threatened by a compliment. He reacts not from the cognitive and rational mind that would allow good reason to accept these positive messages but from a lower state of survival. He becomes emotionally fired up by compliments. He is working to retain what is familiar and safe, even if they are negative and self-defeating. They are what is familiar and safe.

Beliefs Inhibit Academic Performance. For Billy, negative experiences and negative words said to him have created a negative belief system about himself and about the world around him. By school age, he has been hardwired differently than Andy. Negative reactions and harsh punishments in his family created a Billy who is afraid of making mistakes. His natural sense of curiosity and love for learning has become stifled.

To avoid more negativity, Billy will avoid taking healthy risks and will stop trying academics that present even the slightest challenge. Billy's strategy often becomes that of avoiding doing any academic work to avoid embarrassment and shame. He learns to lie, blame, deny, and resist. He can become a master at accomplishing nothing academically despite being in a classroom for six hours.

Mixing a negative belief system with academics can literally be explosive. Parents and teachers report spending hours on one assignment with pencils split in half, papers being torn up, and chairs being thrown. From the adult perspective we think, "It's just a list of spelling words" or "It's just a math worksheet." However, to Billy, that list of spelling words and the worksheet of math problems represent threats to his entire existence. These assignments have the ability to not only remind Billy of his negative beliefs but to confirm their validity beyond a shadow of a doubt.

Although Billy believes he is stupid, he does not really want to feel stupid because this is an uncomfortable and unsettling feeling. When presented with a list of spelling words to alphabetize, he becomes challenged and immediately feels that unwanted sensation of being stupid. If he continues with the list of words and gets them wrong (which he is convinced will happen), then he will be staring at tangible proof that he is genuinely stupid.

The spelling words will prove, once and for all, that he is stupid. In his black-and-white thinking, this is who he is with absolute certainty, with no hope for change. To avoid this outcome, he will resist doing the work. He will fight for hours, refusing to attempt the words, and no threat of any consequence will be enough to overcome this resistance. He will accept the consequence of not going out to recess over feeling stupid. The former has much less weight than the latter.

The issue, then, is not that Billy is being defiant or "lazy." It goes much deeper; it goes to the core of his being. No one wants to feel stupid, especially Billy. The fight is with his belief, not with the spelling words.

Table 5.2. Negative beliefs induced by trauma

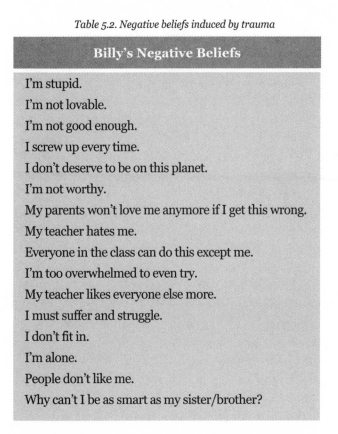

Billy's Negative Beliefs
I'm stupid.
I'm not lovable.
I'm not good enough.
I screw up every time.
I don't deserve to be on this planet.
I'm not worthy.
My parents won't love me anymore if I get this wrong.
My teacher hates me.
Everyone in the class can do this except me.
I'm too overwhelmed to even try.
My teacher likes everyone else more.
I must suffer and struggle.
I don't fit in.
I'm alone.
People don't like me.
Why can't I be as smart as my sister/brother?

Billy may enter the classroom with a plethora of negative beliefs about himself that will interfere with and inhibit his academic performance. A list of these beliefs is listed in Table 5.2. When educators and parents are aware of the magnitude of Billy's resistance to his academics and cease to threaten him with consequences, more effective strategies can be implemented to move Billy out of this negative internal framework. For Billy this means having a voice and feeling heard; using affirmations, mantras, and repetition; and receiving continual support.

Having a Voice. When Billy expresses a negative belief, the adult working with him will typically respond in a way that counteracts this negative belief with a positive belief. If Billy says, "I can't do this. I'm stupid," the teacher usually says, "Billy, that isn't so. You're very smart." Although the intention from the teacher is loving, this type of response invalidates what Billy believes. This contradiction between his belief and the teacher's belief makes him feel even more stupid and frustrated that he is not being heard. Billy does not trust adults to begin with, so if the teacher tries to override her belief with Billy's, the opposite effect happens. It will actually solidify his negative belief.

Billy needs to be able to reprogram his belief system through his own individual process, not by others tacking their beliefs onto him. He needs to feel as if he is being heard. He needs to believe that someone truly understands how he feels, even if it is negative. In order to jump-start the process of changing his belief system, Billy needs acceptance and validation.

Traditionally, the fear was that if Billy expressed himself around this negative belief, it would only serve to strengthen the belief. Quite the opposite is true. Trauma is a result of being powerless and it leaves a child without a voice. Thus, Billy's healing will be found in the moments he is given the chance to have his voice back and to be heard.

Thus, when Billy expresses, "I can't do this. I'm stupid," he needs a validating response such as, "Wow, Billy, that cannot feel good! Explain to me how this makes you feel stupid." Giving Billy the chance to explain why he feels stupid and to have a voice around this feeling is an essential step prior to him changing this belief. Once he is validated—"Billy, I didn't realize this was so big for you and I totally get it now. No wonder you don't want to do this assignment."—the question can be put back out to him of how he can manage to complete the task. "I know it's hard to believe, but I think you're very smart and you can accomplish this. I'm here to help if you need it, so what do you think you can do to still get this list of spelling words in alphabetical order?"

Affirmations. Muhammad Ali was able to create his own reality through affirmations and so can an entire classroom of students. If a computer has corrupt or outdated software, this issue is fixed by upgrading the software. The same is true for the mind. Affirmations are a way to upgrade the negative programming in the mind by replacing it with empowering, positive, and energizing statements.

Most resources will suggest repeating a positive affirmation when sad, depressing, or self-defeating thoughts are present, like saying, "I am happy." However, this is ineffective because you cannot override a negative thought by simply saying something positive—that would be like adding new software to a computer before removing the old corrupted software. It will not work.

For affirmations to be effective, you have to first acknowledge the negative thought, refuse it, and then add the positive. Table 5.3 gives examples of affirmations that can be used to help Billy (and all students) reprogram their beliefs for success and academic achievement.

Mantras. The use of mantras can help children move back quickly to a stable point of reference when they begin to become dysregulated. It is a useful technique to help ground and focus a student back to emotional safety in the heat of the moment.[5] However, when using mantras, preemptive work needs to be done. It is vital to practice and repeat the mantras as a class prior to any behavioral challenges. Then, when an issue arises with Billy, they can be used as a "911" intervention. An example of such mantras would be:

Teacher:	"Who's safe?"
Child:	"I am safe."
Teacher:	"All of the time or some of the time?"
Child:	"All the time!"
Teacher:	"Who is in charge to keep you safe?"
Child:	"You [the teacher] are in charge to keep me safe."
Teacher:	"All of the time or some of the time?"
Child:	"All of the time!"

Repetition. The effectiveness of affirmations and mantras depends greatly on repeating them often. While we all constantly have self-talk going on in our heads, Billy's self-talk is exceptionally negative. Giving him new thoughts at the conscious level and repeating these positive

Table 5.3. Affirmations to reprogram Billy's negative belief system

Positive Affirmations for Classroom Success

Self-Confidence

I refuse to believe I am stupid any longer. I am smart and I accept that now.

I refuse to believe I will fail any longer. I am succeeding and I can do anything I put my mind to. I accept that now.

I refuse to believe I am bad any longer. I am great and I accept that now.

I refuse to believe I am ugly any longer. I am beautiful and I accept that now.

I refuse to believe I am a poor reader any longer. I am a powerful reader and I accept that now.

Emotional

I refuse to believe I am unlovable any longer. I am loved and I am lovable. I accept that now.

I refuse to believe I have to be sad any longer. I am happy and I accept that now.

I refuse to believe I hate myself any longer. I love myself and I accept that now.

Social

I refuse to believe I am disliked any longer. Friends like me and I accept that now.

I refuse to believe I have to work to be liked any longer. Friends like me just the way I am and I accept that now.

thoughts daily will eventually embed them at the subconscious level. Muhammad Ali is credited to have said, "It's the repetition of affirmations that leads to belief. And once that belief becomes a deep conviction, things begin to happen."

When children learn their times tables, it takes practicing them over and over. The basic process for learning anything new is to first be introduced to the material then to transfer the information from short-term memory to long-term memory. The same is true for helping children to get out of their negative belief systems. This can be accomplished by being in an environment that is continually supporting them in a positive, affirming way, while at the same time giving them emotional space to discharge the old beliefs.

When Nothing Seems to Work. There will be times when no matter what positive supports are put into place, no matter what encouraging environment is established, and no matter how strong a relationship Billy has with his teachers, he will continue to struggle. Due to the chaotic and difficult lifestyle Billy has had in the past, his belief system says that he must suffer, fight, and struggle. His subconscious mind will work to sabotage and it will work to make his life difficult. Crisis is his modus operandi.

When the obstacles are taken out of the way, Billy will then create the obstacles. He does not believe he is entitled to peace, happiness, and an easy road. Although at a conscious level, he is tired of the struggle, he continues to create the struggle at an unconscious level. It is a terrible dichotomic state in which to live.

When nothing else can be done, it will simply take continuing with the parameters that are in place for Billy and allowing him to struggle. This has to be his process; healing cannot be forced. Keep the boundaries strong and clear, allowing Billy to have something to "push against" to know that the supports and people around him are strong enough to lovingly handle him.

CHAPTER SIX

Ask the Right Questions

■

Asking the right questions takes as much skill
as giving the right answers.
~ Robert Half

I f you ask the right questions, you will get the right answers. Hence, if you ask the wrong questions, you will similarly get the wrong answers. Wrong answers come from wrong questions.

Billy has continually struggled in the classroom, received detention after detention, failed repeatedly at his academics, and has been painfully ostracized socially, all because we have been asking the wrong question. When seeing Billy struggling, we have asked, "How do I get Billy to change his behavior?" This is the wrong question because Billy's struggle isn't behaviorally based. The root of his struggle goes much deeper than him simply making a better and more mindful decision to consciously behave.

As seen in previous chapters, Billy's struggle is based in development, trauma, beliefs, and regulation. Developmentally, he has gaps and deficits that prevent him from being able to make sense of his world. His early traumatic experiences keep him in a place to react instantly to anything he perceives as threatening, whether real or imagined. He believes he is stupid, unworthy, and unlovable. His compromised regulatory system prevents him from being able to self-soothe and calm back down on his own when his system becomes aroused.

Working to change Billy's behavior when the root of the problem is not really behavior can prove maddening for both the teacher and Billy. It is like going up to bat and striking out for the entire season.

First Question. It is time to change the question. What we need to be asking is:

"What is driving Billy's behavior?"

There is always a reason behind a child's behavioral responses. When we can get to the reason and to the root of what is driving the behavior, the doors open to finding solutions that not only change behavior but also offer amazing long-term change and healing for students.

Here is a true story of a student at a special needs school who was working to solve his regulatory issues while the teachers and staff saw it only as a behavioral issue:

Billy began to get restless and agitated in class. In the past, he would act out and become aggressive toward the teacher and students, throwing objects and pushing other students. After several times of getting in trouble for this, he expressed to his mom that he was trying to change his behavior because he did not want to be "bad" anymore and did not want any points taken off his point chart. One day, his agitation kept building and when his teacher noticed him, she reminded him that he needed to sit up, get back to his work, and refocus; otherwise, she would be taking points off of his point chart. But the more he tried to sit still, the more frustrated he became. He felt as if an internal volcano inside of him was building and it was going to erupt to the point he would not be able to control himself. Knowing it was wrong to hit and revert to old behaviors but with no other clear options, he ran out of the classroom and bolted to the library. Swinging the library door open, he bypassed the librarian and ran to his favorite section of storybooks. He hastily pulled out three books, found a comfortable reading spot in the corner of the library, and started reading his books. The librarian, noticing this whirlwind of activity, realized that Billy did not have a pass from his teacher to enter the library. She went over to reprimand him and proceeded to take the books away saying, "Billy, you can't just come in here and pull books off the shelves without permission. That is NOT allowed. Give me those books now." As she went to take the books away from Billy, he lost all sense of self-control and began hitting and kicking the librarian.

This example shows the limitations of asking the wrong question. The teacher was approaching Billy in a manner in which to answer the question, "How do I get Billy to change his behavior?" There was no acknowledgment of the dysregulation that was building up inside of Billy. Asking him to behave at that moment was like putting a Band-Aid on the outside of a wound that is bleeding internally.

When we look closer at what Billy was doing, we realize that his activity was a regulatory issue, not a behavioral issue. Reading was a way to help Billy calm down. Billy knew that sitting and reading a book would provide him the regulatory activity he needed to settle his anxiety and his nervous system. He was not intentionally being defiant. Conversely, he was intentionally seeking to find a way to behave by regulating himself.

Although it was against the rules for him to run out of the room, Billy actually had more cognitive thinking going on inside of him than what was acknowledged. He made a decision not to hit and become aggressive. He was able to think of an alternative activity that created regulation for him: reading. His plan of action was actually brilliant; it is just that it was against the rules.

This kind of misunderstanding is painful. We have a student who is working to the best of his ability to solve his regulatory issues and a teacher and librarian who are working to the best of their abilities to keep a child safe, ensuring he follows the rules, and are trying to maintain order in the school, all to no avail.

The solution lies in asking the question, "What is driving Billy's behavior?" When we understand Billy's perspective, we have the right answer: Billy is seeking to regulate when he becomes upset. We need to teach Billy how to regulate instead of trying to teach him why it is wrong to run out of the classroom and why he cannot be allowed in the library without a pass. In fact, Billy has actually solved the problem for us. He is showing us that reading helps him regulate. Instead of punishing his ingenuity and creativity, we need to appreciate it and use it as part of the solution. This can be done while simultaneously getting him to follow the basic rules of the school.

The teacher could lovingly approach Billy and suggest they work out a way for Billy to have "book time" when he needed it. A schedule could be set up that worked with the teacher's schedule or Billy could be given the chance to express his need to regulate when he became dysregulated in the future, without having to go into flight mode and leave the classroom. If Billy were to feel supported and understood, free of threats and fear, the need to leave the classroom would be completely alleviated.

This is just one solution of how Billy's need to regulate and the teacher's need for him to obey the rules can come together successfully. With an openness of understanding of what is driving Billy's behavior, a plethora of appropriate solutions is available.

Sometimes, however, the primary question—"What is driving Billy's behavior?"—may leave the teacher stumped, and the answer may need further exploration. More specific questions that dive deeper and at a slightly different angle may be necessary to answer this primary question. Go deeper and try asking these more detailed exploratory questions:

- What else is really going on here?
- What does this child need?
- How can I change my perspective?
- What keeps me only looking at the behavior?
- What is this behavior communicating right now?
- What in the environment could be triggering this behavior?

In the prior library example, if we ask the question, "What is this behavior saying?" we need to be cautious not to answer it with traditional thinking. Traditional thinking would say, "He is running out of the classroom because he refuses to follow the rules and he refuses to have anyone in charge of him." Instead, answer the question with a regulatory framework. "He is running out of the classroom because he is about to hit his breaking point and he is seeking a self-soothing activity in order to rebuild his window of stress tolerance."

Here is how the other exploratory questions could be answered:

- *What else is really going on here?* Billy is overwhelmed being in a classroom with all the other students; the library offers peace and solitude, which is safety.

- *What does this child need?* He needs a regulated adult to help him calm back down instead of threats that points will be taken off his point chart.

- *How can I change my perspective?* I need to put aside the fear of an entire school going into chaos if every student were to simply run out of the classroom. I need to look into the eyes of the student and see things from his perspective. I need to "feel" what it is like for him to be on his own trying to deal with an overabundance of internal emotional reactivity.

- *What keeps me only looking at the behavior?* I am scared of appearing like the type of teacher who cannot control her students. I do not want to be judged but want to be regarded as the teacher who has it together and her students respect her.

- *What is this behavior communicating right now?* Billy is very stressed.

- *What in the environment could be triggering this behavior?* Let me look at what happened moments prior to Billy getting agitated. Something could have been building up to this final moment, which I can help to interrupt and calm in the future.

Second Question. Traditionally, we have viewed the teacher-student relationship in a strict hierarchical fashion: "I am the teacher; you are the student. You will do as I say and you will learn what I teach." This one-way-street philosophy may have worked in years past, but it is only marginally effective today, even with our Andys.

We live in a different world—a more conscious and sophisticated world that demands a higher level of reciprocal respect and mutual understanding with both adults and children. Even large corporations are realizing that this top-down control system of the past does not provide the profitability it once did.

In his book, *Delivering Happiness,* Tony Hsieh, CEO of the online retailer Zappos, describes how he built his company on the principle of service. Grossing over $1 billion in merchandise sales annually, Zappos proved that a different, more humane perspective could produce outcomes of grand proportion. One of the core values that led to his company's amazing success was, and continues to be, the concept of service.[1]

At Zappos, this concept of service was developed not only for customers but as an internal core value of the entire company, with a top-down attitude of service. Hsieh writes: "The best leaders are servant-leaders. They serve those they lead."[2]

Service begins with empathy; empathy is putting yourself in the shoes of the other person. When you open yourself up to the other person's pain, fear, and overwhelm, you have a deeper understanding as to their needs and how you can help them. Empathy is when you give up judgment for understanding.

This service attitude is not new. Martin Luther King, Jr., said, "Everyone has the power for greatness, not for fame, because greatness is determined by service." Yet this philosophy of service, within the framework of empathy, has not been globally incorporated into our schools, especially with difficult and challenging children. In fact, it has been students like Billy (the most misunderstood, mislabeled, and misperceived students who constantly struggle to understand this world) that traditionally have been given the least amount of empathy. It is easy to give Andy empathy when he is upset, but it is much more challenging to give Billy empathy when he is upset. Andy offers an invitation to come and connect and is ripe to receive empathy. Billy, on the other hand, is pulsating negative energy directly at you and is ready to resist you at any moment.

Imagine a radical new approach where the teacher, principal, or parent has a "How may I serve you?" attitude toward Billy, just as was Tony Hsieh's philosophy as CEO. How would this affect Billy's response system? Consider for a moment a change in your paradigm and the possibility of embracing a new mindset where students are your customers. This type of shift in perspective reinforces the core goal that this model is working to accomplish with each student: relationship.

So the second question to ask yourself during every interaction with Billy, especially when you are stumped by the first question is:

"What can I do at this very moment to improve my relationship with this student?"

Instead of focusing at the moment on how to change Billy's behavior or instill a life lesson about right verses wrong, approaching Billy initially through the context of the relationship will work to get to the core of the issue. Again, the core issue is not behavior; it is stemming from a developmental deficiency, traumatic experience, negative belief system, or regulatory inability. At the moment of the negative behavior, this is the time when Billy is least likely to be able to think clearly, make good decisions, or think about the consequences of his actions.

Here is a list of more detailed and exploratory questions to consider when working to answer the second question: "What can I do at this very moment to improve my relationship with this student?"

- How can I make this relationship safe for Billy?
- Does Billy need me to validate him?
- What does Billy need from me?
- How can I respond so Billy is not threatened?
- How can I physically position myself to create safety in relationship for Billy? Can I sit down or squat to be less threatening but not in harm's way?
- Can Billy respond to exploratory questions, not solutions I give him, that show I am interested?
- How can I convince Billy that I truly want to understand his struggle?
- How can I be more authentic for Billy?
- If I stop talking and start listening, will Billy feel like he has a voice?
- How can I serve Billy?

The following example, where one therapist was able to successfully connect with Billy at the relationship level, puts this into real life:

On a hot day, Billy (a fourth grader) was in the courtyard with seven other classmates playing. When it came time to line up and return to the classroom, the teacher noticed that Billy was not lining up. Instead, Billy became obstinate and refused to move. Standing there, as if he was glued to the ground, he kept repeating, "I need some water." The teacher responded, "Billy, we'll get water once you line up. You need to line up now." Billy refused to respond and continued looping, "I need some water. I need some water…." The teacher pulled out her clipboard and said, "Billy, I'm taking a point off your point chart right now." Billy, unfazed by this action, continued, "I need some water."

The school therapist, who had Billy on her caseload, was walking by and noticed this unfolding of events. The therapist knew Billy's history. He was currently living with his aunt because his biological parents were unable to care for him and he had experienced intense neglect when he was younger. Police found Billy roaming the streets of the red light district early one morning at two years old, unkempt, unfed, and unsupervised. Billy had a massive history around not having enough food and water. At this point, the therapist asked if she could take Billy out of the courtyard and work with him. The teacher, in complete exhaustion, said, "Yes … take him!"

The therapist came over to Billy and gently said, "You're going to be okay. Come with me." Instead of mentioning Billy's disobedience and refusal to follow the rules, she addressed the core of the issue going on with Billy: safety. She recognized that Billy had been triggered back to a time in his history where he felt like he was going to die without water. He needed relationship and reassurance before he needed points taken off of his point chart.

The therapist reassured Billy she was there to make sure he was safe and taken care of. She walked him to the water fountain and helped him take some deep breaths to calm down. Once he was calm, she spoke to him about the necessity of getting back into line with his class and following the teacher's instructions. Once this incident was over, Billy was able to finish out the rest of the school day without a single point being taken off of his point chart, which was unusual even on a good day for Billy.

To successfully answer the question, "What can I do at this very moment to improve my relationship with this student?" it takes trusting in the process to be able to ignore the behavior in the beginning. Remember, Billy cannot learn when he is stressed out. It is a matter of timing as to when to teach the lesson.

It also takes allowing yourself to not take Billy's behavior personally or as disrespect to you as the authority figure. Billy is in a state of survival. When a child (or adult) is in this state, no one else matters. It is a mindset about protecting the self. A teacher's ability to be "successful" with Billy comes through her ability to connect with him, despite her own internal reactions. Love is about taking the higher road; that is the true response of the person with authority.

By connecting with Billy at the level of relationship, the teacher will be working to calm his fears, soothe his stress, and decrease his overwhelm. Once Billy has moved back into a state of regulation, shifted into the neocortex, and expanded his window of stress tolerance, then the issue at hand can be addressed and with more effectiveness.

Table 6.1 shows both the first and second questions to ask Billy along with more detailed and exploratory questions.

Responding to Students. Teaching a student like Billy requires a more sensitive approach. It takes responding to Billy instead of reacting to him. His system is hardwired at a higher set point and he perceives most of what is said to him as negative and threatening. The long-term goal is to help Billy lower his reactivity and shift his system back down to what is seen in Andy. However, we must meet Billy where he is at, in the present moment. It is within the process of every

interaction, meeting Billy with sensitivity, reassurance, and love that
we are able to help him build a stronger and more secure foundation.
When Billy feels safe, supported, and listened to, his ability to focus,
organize, and learn has the potential to expand exponentially.

Table 6.1. The first and second questions along with their exploratory questions

The Right Questions to Ask

1. What is driving this student's behavior?

- What else is really going on here?
- What does this child need?
- How can I change my perspective?
- What keeps me only looking at the behavior?
- What is this behavior communicating right now?
- What in the environment could be triggering this behavior?

2. What can I do at this very moment to improve my relationship with this student?

- How can I make this relationship safe for Billy?
- Does Billy need me to validate him?
- What does Billy need from me?
- How can I respond so Billy is not threatened?
- How can I physically position myself to create safety in relationship for Billy? Can I sit down or squat to be less threatening but not in harm's way?
- Can Billy respond to exploratory questions, not solutions I give him, that show I am interested?
- How can I convince Billy that I truly want to understand his struggle?
- How can I be more authentic for Billy?
- If I stop talking and start listening, will Billy feel like he has a voice?
- How can I serve Billy?

This importance of responding, not reacting, to Billy cannot be overemphasized. Rebuilding his foundation and his perception of the school environment is an absolute necessity. As mentioned in chapter 4, if you were going to build a thirteen-story building, you could not start on the fifth floor. You have to have a strong foundation in order to reach the top floor without collapse.

The process of responding instead of reacting to students like Billy begins with putting yourself in Billy's shoes. He feels alone, different, unlovable, unworthy, overwhelmed, and stupid. Table 6.2 gives examples of ways we have traditionally reacted to Billy through the eyes of an adult compared to how we should respond to Billy through the eyes of Billy.

Students, especially students like Billy, need their teachers and caregivers to go beyond consequences, logic, and control. They need the adults in their lives to connect with them in relationship. Through their misbehaviors, they are seeking external regulation. These behaviors serve a purpose. For children like Billy, they know only a few misguided strategies in which to seek regulation. Replacing punishment with relationship through loving responses, as shown in Table 6.2, is one of the most effective strategies in helping children like Billy in the long term.

When we react in traditional ways, the reality is that we are teaching Billy more of the same types of behaviors he is already exhibiting. We are continuing the cycle of reactivity. The way to change challenging students in the classroom is through influence, not control. No one on this planet likes to be controlled, especially Billy. Influencing Billy through the power of the relationship by providing emotional safety, empathy, connection, tolerance, kindness, security, and acceptance is what it is going to take to get out of the strenuous loop on negative behavior in the classroom. We have to trust that, fundamentally at their core, children are acting out due to stress, fear, and a lack of regulatory ability.

The most effective moment in a student's day to teach him a new pattern is precisely in the most difficult moment of his day. This is when he has reverted back to old patterns, old thinking, and old coping strategies. Addressing Billy in the context of relationship in the middle of the storm is where lasting change happens. Change the pattern of what he experiences in the context of relationship instead

Table 6.2. Examples of changing traditional reactions to beyond consequences responses

Responding Instead of Reacting	
Traditional Reactions	**Beyond Consequences Responses**
"It's not that difficult."	"I need to know how hard this is for you."
"Go to the principal's office."	"I'm here. You're not in trouble."
"You're a teenager now and you need to learn to deal with life."	"I don't want you alone in this. Let me help you."
"Stop crying."	"It's okay to feel."
"You're so dramatic."	"You need to be heard."
"Stop acting like a baby."	"That really set you back, didn't it?"
"Detention is waiting for you."	"Sit with me."
"Stop being so needy."	"What is it you need help with?"
"You need to learn to be responsible."	"Let's chunk this down so it is more manageable."
"I can't help you with this issue—I've got thirty other children in this classroom."	"We'll get through this together. Every single student in this class is important."
"Don't you talk to an adult like that!"	"You're allowed to have a voice. Let's talk together."
"Stop whining."	"I want to understand you better. If I know how you feel, I'll be able to help you better. Use your voice so I can really understand."
"You should never have acted like that."	"Sometimes life just gets too big, doesn't it?"
"I'm calling your parents. Wait until they find out."	"Let's get everyone involved to support you. You're not in trouble. I want your parents involved so we can all find a way to make this better."
"Act your age."	"This is too big to keep to yourself."

Responding Instead of Reacting	
Traditional Reactions	**Beyond Consequences Responses**
"You need to take ownership/ responsibility for this."	"I'm sorry this is so hard."
"You're old enough to handle this on your own."	"Let's handle this together."
"Grow up."	"I'm here to support you."
"You won't have help in college, so you need to do this on your own now."	"Let me help you now so you'll be ready for college."
"You need to behave because you're in my classroom."	"I am here to make it safe for you."
"You need to be like Andy."	"You have your own kind of genius."
"Nobody is going to like you if you keep misbehaving."	"I know you want to be well liked, so let's make that happen."

of trying to change the way he is thinking. Interrupt the present behavior in the most difficult moment and there lies the greatest chance of permanently changing future behavior.

This Feels Like I'm Coddling Billy. Yes, at first, it will feel like you are "giving in," "coddling," and "babying" Billy. This interpretation is stemming from the traditional viewpoint that students simply misbehave out of choice. However, students act out because they need attention. Ignoring the behavior, threatening the behavior, or controlling the behavior will only give the child a form of negative attention. This is extremely detrimental because from a child's viewpoint any form of attention—whether positive or negative—is attention, and it is ultimately interpreted as love by the child. When working to connect with Billy to meet his needs instead of trying to control him, peaceful and loving outcomes can unfold naturally, as illustrated in the following true story:

Billy ran out of his fourth-grade classroom and down the hall where he climbed under a table that was partially enclosed. The teacher's aide from the class ran after Billy and was joined by another nearby staff member. The two of them surrounded the table as Billy screamed for them to go away and leave him alone. The principal, with whom Billy had a strong trusting relationship, came to see what all the yelling was about and motioned the two staff members back to their classroom while she stayed to attend to Billy.

The principal stood quietly against the wall about ten feet from the table. After a few minutes of silence, Billy shouted, "I know you're there! I can see your feet!" The principal calmly replied, "I'm just here to love you" and said nothing else.

Once the principal said these words, Billy's entire demeanor changed. The principal knew that students were about to move into the hallway who would be transitioning to another class, so the principal asked Billy if he would like to walk over to the next room with her where there was a comfy chair and she could hold him for a few moments. Billy crawled out from the table and went with the principal. It took only a few moments of holding Billy on her lap and comforting him until he was regulated enough to ask to go back to class.

While each school will have its own policy on holding children, simply connecting and offering to hold Billy's hand could easily accomplish the same outcome described in this story. The staff perceived the principal as "coddling" Billy, but had the principal not intervened in this manner Billy surely would have gone into fight mode if he had been forced from underneath the table (Billy's safe zone he had created). It will take throwing out these old perceptions and embracing the truth about children: They need attention, nurturing, and relationship in order to stay within the boundaries, to follow rules, and to stay attentive to the teacher in charge of them. Billy needs the adults in charge of him to reduce his stress, increase his regulation, and provide an emotionally safe and secure environment.

At the same time, Billy also needs to be given strong boundaries to "push up against" to know he is safe and that the people around him can handle him. It is as if he needs a hybrid between Mister Rogers and General George Patton—someone holding strong limits and boundaries (General Patton) but presenting them with softness and compassion (Mister Rogers).

© The Fred Rogers Company,
used with permission.

© Bettmann/CORBIS,
used with permission.

Figure 6.1. The combination of Mister Rogers and General George Patton is needed for Billy.

It will take repeating these experiences over and over in the classroom to change Billy's brain, his thinking, and his patterning. For a child like Billy, his neural networks are woven together in chaos. Thus, it takes patterned, predictable, and repetitive experiences with a loving and regulated teacher to calm his brain and reprogram his mind. Billy has a chance to be more like Andy; he simply needs the "coddling," attention, and sensitivity his brain is needing, demanding, and craving. Trust in the plasticity of the human nervous system, give him these, and see the miracles that can happen.

As Willa Cather wrote, "Where there is great love, there are always miracles."

PART TWO

The Beyond Consequences Classroom

CHAPTER SEVEN

Motivation

■

Sometimes even to live is an act of courage.
~ Lucius Annaeus Seneca

M otivation is a nebulous and magical force that drives people to initiate behaviors geared toward the accomplishment of goals. It is a "call to action" that is supposed to be naturally activated at every age and every developmental stage. Students like Andy are naturally motivated by an instinctual sense of curiosity. They are curious about the world and have an unbridled love for learning.

Trauma robs a child of his sense of curiosity. When the world and the people around Billy are no longer safe, his sense of curiosity becomes locked down, severely hindering his internal sense of motivation. It is a fear response. The mindset shifts 180 degrees and the traumatized child now thinks, "If I don't explore, initiate, or put forth effort, then I am safe."

One theory used to explain the nature of human motivation is the arousal theory. This theory suggests there is an internal thermometer that is perpetually activated to balance out levels of arousal. If the arousal level decreases, then a person will look for excitement such as physical exercise or a nightclub. When the opposite occurs and the arousal level is too high, this same person will seek down time, as in reading a book or watching a movie.

For Billy, his internal arousal level is stuck on high, whether he is hyperactive in his behavior or on the quiet, shut-down side. He was not properly regulated in his past to be able to have a more "normal" set point like Andy. Since his high arousal level is due to fear, he will be ever seeking to bring his arousal down by creating safety.

Unfortunately, we have traditionally viewed this child as resistant and lazy, void of motivation.

Traditional View

Traditionally, it has been believed that a student's level of motivation is influenced by several factors: (1) the need to have approval from others, (2) the desire to overcome challenges, (3) an interest in the subject matter, (4) a general desire to achieve, (5) self-confidence, and (6) persistence. For Andy, a student who enters the classroom relatively regulated and having an internal sense of "I'm okay," these factors hold true. Billy has not yet come to the level of feeling physically or emotionally safe in the classroom. Therefore, he is still at the lower levels of the hierarchy of learning. Whether or not the subject being taught is of interest is irrelevant.

External rewards have been regarded as solutions to help students who do not naturally have a strong sense of internal motivation. Positive rewards, such as those listed in Table 7.1, are typical external motivators. Andy can successfully respond to these rewards. With Billy, a much different result unfolds.

Table 7.1. Typical external positive and negative motivators

Positive Motivators	Negative Motivators
Sticker charts	Alienation
Homework coupons	Suspension
Class parties	Extra homework
Extra free time	Yelling
Fun Fridays	Missing extracurricular activities
Treasure box prizes	Summer school
Food and treats	Time-outs

In Billy's quest for the reward, even one that would be considered a positive motivator, like stickers or a prize from the treasure box, stress is created. He wants the reward but collapses under the stress created to earn it. The stakes are high and unmanageable within his window of stress tolerance. His exaggerated black-and-white perspective tells him that if he does not get the reward, then he is stupid, bad, unlovable, different, unworthy, and unsuccessful. He does not have the regulatory ability to handle the overwhelming feelings this creates; hence, he acts out and demonstrates negative defeating behaviors. Such positive motivators often backfire for students like Billy.

Negative motivators, such as the threat of alienation, have traditionally been used as a means to get students to be participatory and to complete assignments. Placing students in the corner, having them sit beside the teacher (as a punishment), or exiting students out of the classroom to sit in the hallway by themselves are prime examples. Unfortunately, these only create division and labeling between students, as well as stress for Billy.

> **SURVEY SAYS:**
>
> ---
>
> "I got sent out of the classroom all the time. One time I didn't want to leave the classroom and be in the hallway alone so I knocked a chair over and wouldn't go."

Andy is motivated to behave because Andy does not want to be "bad" like Billy. Billy, who has a history of abandonment and rejection, gets isolated, which confirms his internal belief that he really is a bad child. As a result, his negative behavior increases in severity. Ironically he creates exactly what he feared from the start.

The traditional school environment has been structured in a rigid hierarchical system to keep students in line and motivated: "I am the teacher. You are the student. I will teach you. You will listen and you will learn." While it is appropriate and absolutely necessary to have

> **SURVEY SAYS:**
>
> ---
>
> "A nice teacher would make school better. I had one in 3rd grade and I never got in trouble. In 4th grade I had a teacher who kept putting me out of the classroom and I couldn't stand that."

this hierarchy in the classroom, the reality is that it has been taken to the extreme and often leaves no room for relationship.

Billy, who has a history of being hurt and traumatized by those in charge of him, will resist this type of structure in order to ensure his safety. He does not trust adults, and rightfully so; his history tells him not to. To adapt to this type of hierarchy in the classroom, Billy must feel emotionally safe first. Developing a strong and loving relationship with the teacher and other adult leaders will be critical to his ability to take his place as a student with the teacher in charge.

New View

Children have a natural love for learning. As young toddlers, they learn to crawl and walk without external motivators. Certainly they like encouragement, but the natural desire to progress is already a part of their innate programming. Children do not need to be bribed or threatened into learning. What they need, especially Billy, is to be supported, guided, and scaffolded up within an environment that is conducive to feeling emotionally safe, developing relationship, and feeling respected.

The traditional techniques invented and implemented in the past, as discussed in the prior paragraphs, are barriers and hindrances to Billy's progression because they create fear. Any technique based in fear is only going to elevate more fear in Billy who already lives in fear. These techniques are like wolves in sheep's clothing; they are illusions. The reality is that when fear is a part of the learning environment for a child like Billy, learning stops. What subsequently follows is exactly what these external motivators were intended to eliminate: negative behaviors.

Motivation is more about regulation than about simply making a choice to succeed and follow the rules. Traditional techniques like stickers and rewards address the area of the brain that is shut down for Billy. To think clearly and to sequentially rationalize that "if I behave, then I will have a prize from the treasure box" takes the work of the neocortex. For Billy, when he is struggling and dysregulated, this part of the brain ceases to fire (see chapter 3). The problem exists in the lower area of the brain for Billy. That is why his thinking is going to be different than Andy's, especially because his negative belief system says that he is stupid, the world is unsafe, and he has to do whatever it takes to make things work for himself (see Figure 7.1).

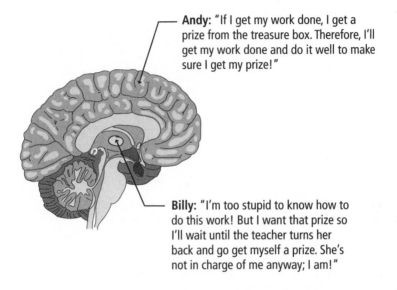

Andy: "If I get my work done, I get a prize from the treasure box. Therefore, I'll get my work done and do it well to make sure I get my prize!"

Billy: "I'm too stupid to know how to do this work! But I want that prize so I'll wait until the teacher turns her back and go get myself a prize. She's not in charge of me anyway; I am!"

Figure 7.1. Top-down thinking vs. bottom-up thinking.

In the lower part of the brain, life happens in the next fifteen seconds. Consequences are not relevant. Morals, ethics, and the differences between "right and wrong" have no bearing. All of these guiding forces reside in the neocortex, an area of the brain no longer "in charge" when Billy is dysregulated.

The solution requires interactive regulation (through relationship) to calm Billy down, to create safety for Billy, and to decrease his anxiety. It takes switching from the strategy of getting students motivated—with the promise of a reward or the threat of the loss of a privilege—to the strategy that taps into the student's neurobiological predisposition for relationship. Tap into the need for co-regulation and you will see amazing results, as seen in the following example:

An elementary school teacher switched from using the well-known "Red Light Classroom Management" plan to one that

*addresses a child's need for safety and regulation. In this Red
Light plan, each child begins the day with a green light. As
negative behaviors and choices are made, the child then
digresses to a yellow light and ultimately to a red light, with
each level having a consequence attached to it. Instead, this
teacher created a program based on the kangaroo's safe
pocket, which replaced the green light. Each student started
the day with a kangaroo in a pocket that had his name on it.
When a student acted out, the student's kangaroo would be
transferred over to the teacher's safe pouch, demonstrating
that the student needed to feel safe and needed the teacher's
help in getting regulated. She explained to the students that
her number one job was to keep everyone safe and feeling
secure in her classroom. This way, anyone needing extra
support was given exactly that, free of punishment or fear.
The system was much more effective in teaching students
appropriate behaviors because she was able to help regulate
students and shift them back to a place of safety and security.[1]*

This approach is brilliant for a student like Billy because it helps
him shift out of fear-and-survival mode. When Billy is left to his own
devices to regulate, all his internal resources and energy are already
used for protection and safety, leaving no room for learning. The more
Billy falls behind academically, the more he feels threatened and the
less he learns. Hence, the negative and endless spiral begins with no
way out when traditional approaches are put into place. Unfortunately,
the only way out of this downward spiral for many students is to
ultimately quit and drop out of school.

It takes a shift from a behavioral perspective to a relationship-based
regulatory perspective to interrupt a child's negative spiral downward.
Many of the traditional techniques need only be modified slightly and
delivered in the spirit of love and connection (as in the example above)
rather than in the framework of fear and control. It is a small shift yet
one that can have a powerful impact on students.

Create a Sense of Belonging. Under natural conditions,
humans have historically lived in multigenerational and multicultural
settings. The human species has long been defined by groups and by

the nuclear family. In fact, we are biologically designed to be in community. It goes against our nervous system to be isolated, and studies show that our physical health is dependent on the quality of our relationships. We all need to belong and feel like we are important to others.

When a student senses that others think, "You are one of us," safety is inherently created. Unfortunately, traditional classroom responses to Billy's negative behaviors do exactly the opposite. Traditional consequences of isolating and alienating are relational expressions that say, "You are not one of us." With these traditional techniques, Billy is marginalized in his own classroom community. This type of disciplinary action will ignite Billy's stress response system further because he has a history of being rejected, abandoned, or targeted as the bad child. His past memories dictate how the present moment will be interpreted. He is triggered by this sense of not belonging and it sends him into a panic. A student's past family history is critical to understanding his present state and reaction in the classroom.

Create a sense of belonging not just for the Billys in the classroom but for all students by focusing on the class as a community. The class is the "family" that supports, understands, tolerates, validates, and loves each student in his individual differences (instead of expecting each student to be the same and fit into a predefined mold). The entire class should exist for the needs of each student, not the other way around (where traditionally the students exist for the needs of

> **SURVEY SAYS:**
>
> "You should have the freedom to be yourself without the fear of being judged."

the class). When one student is dysregulated, the class stops to support this one student and everyone works to help this student feel safe. It is the coming together of everyone to support the needs of the one.

It may seem like this would take too much time and would interrupt academic progression. In the beginning, it will take more time and the academics probably will be second in line. Reading, writing, and arithmetic are important but so is relationship. Once safety, security, and acceptance are solidified at the beginning of the school year, such an environment will progress academic learning to its highest potential over the span of the entire school year. It is the investment of time and emotional energy where the payoff materializes into academic achievement long term.

A community atmosphere helps to empower every student and gives each student a voice, as shown in the following example:

> *In one classroom, a teacher was able to establish this type of family-oriented learning environment. When a student got dysregulated, everyone was able to join in to help this student feel safe again. The teacher had a singing bowl and when Billy became dysregulated one day, another student rang the singing bowl (which he was given permission to do) and called out, "Everyone just breathe!" The teacher at this point was able to say, "We all need to stop. Pause. Breathe. We're all okay and everyone is safe." The teacher then encouraged the students to continue what they were doing and went over to Billy and helped to individually regulate him in order to get back on task. The class continued on in their work and Billy was able to quickly shift back on track.*

At Watershed School, an innovative school in Boulder, Colorado, students meet at a set time once a week for what they have termed "advisory." One teacher is designated as the "advisor" and is assigned to each advisory group of students in various grades. The group stays intact for all four years, from ninth grade through graduation. Each advisory group grows to become more like a tight-knit family, where students have an emotionally safe place to discuss any issue that comes up in their lives. It is a place for students to work out social, emotional, and academic issues. Each member of the advisory has a voice and is given an equal chance to be heard and understood every week.

SURVEY SAYS:

"Yes, I liked school because I had the best teacher ever and she helped my class become a family."

The result is a school with students who have a greater level of trust and security, with a decrease in negative social issues. Students learn to communicate better at all levels, and the ability to say "I need help" improves. The teachers understand each student better, which directly transposes to an increase in academic achievement. The one-hour-a-week time investment, along with the emotional and relational investment given by each advisor, has proven to benefit the school tremendously.

When programs like this one at Watershed School can be delivered in a relational and community-oriented way, students feel safe. When they feel like they belong, academic achievement happens. Here are some more simple yet effective ways for students to feel like they truly belong to the classroom community:

> ### SURVEY SAYS:
>
> "My suggestion is that the environment is comforting, and friendly. No student wants to sit in a classroom that just has desks, and chairs."

- Take time to talk to and acknowledge each student. When the student walks into the classroom, convey the message, "Welcome. This class would not be the same without you here today!"
- Recognize the students' moods and help to regulate instead of ignoring or criticizing the moods.
- Listen to the students (you don't have to agree—just listen).
- Smile at the students and stay in a warm place in your heart, no matter their attitude or disposition.
- Take an interest in what is important to each student.
- Ask the students for help and let the students help.
- Keep an attitude of "You're always welcome here."
- Share the student's idea with others ("Billy had a good idea for....").

Create a Classroom Designed for Regulation. For students to be motivated, they have to be regulated. You cannot have one without the other. Therefore, the classroom should be set up to assist in keeping students regulated throughout the school day or class period.

Movement. Repetitive motor movement can be key in helping some students regulate. Patterned, rhythmic, and repetitive movements settle the brain and activate the vestibular system (the sensory system that responds to movement and our sense of balance). When a baby is upset, the caregiver either rocks, bounces, or sways with the baby to calm the baby down. The same is true for older children. These types of movements should be encouraged in the classroom to settle children, help them regain their focus, and open up the pathways for more learning. Here are some ideas to offer movement for children:

- *Rocking.* Rocking taps into the memory of being safe. Have a rocking chair in the classroom for children to either rock on their own or offer to rock younger children.

- *Pacing.* We naturally pace when we are anxious. It is a way for the body to regulate. The neocortex can absorb more information while the body is moving compared to sitting still. Mark off a pacing track in the back of the classroom with tape and allow students to pace even if you are presenting an academic lesson. Billy will learn better when he is free to move instead of being forced to sit still, which will create the feeling of being trapped.

- *Standing exercises.* As a class, incorporate exercises each student can do standing up at his desk. Brain Gym® movements can significantly increase students' abilities to concentrate and focus.

- *Sitting exercises.* Fitness balls can be excellent alternatives to chairs for children who need to have their bodies moving while seated at their desks.

- *Movement through space.* Activities, such as spinning and swinging, can help to regulate a child both physically and emotionally. Playground equipment, such as slides and merry-go-rounds, offer children a playful and fun way to reregulate.

- *Bilateral activities.* Two-sided, or bilateral, activities such as jumping rope, crawling, and riding a bike are excellent movements to help balance the body.

Children often do things that demonstrate the exact solutions needed to help them. It is up to the adults to see the solutions being presented instead of seeing only the breaking of the rules. The following example shows how a child knew that movement was what he needed to get regulated but was breaking the rules in the process:

Billy would become upset in the classroom and run out without asking permission from his teacher. Each time, he would run to the school elevator and "play" inside the elevator by sending it up and down to the two floors repeatedly. He would refuse to come out and only wanted to make the elevator go up and down, up and down. The teachers talked to Billy on several occasions to help him understand that the elevator was not a toy but a necessary piece of equipment for many of the handicapped students. They explained that he was not allowed to run out of the classroom, as leaving the class without adult supervision was against the classroom rules. Billy was told he would receive demerits each time he ran to the elevator. This scenario happened multiple times throughout the school year, yet no amount of explaining seemed to influence Billy's behavior. No amount of demerits had any effect on him. It appeared as if Billy would make up his mind and do what he wanted whether it was against the rules or not.

What Billy was doing clearly revealed a regulatory issue, not a behavioral issue, yet the teachers were asking, "How do I get Billy to change his behavior?" which is the wrong question. The movement of the elevator, going up and down, was providing a sensory experience at the physiological level to help regulate Billy. He was not intentionally being defiant. Conversely, he was intentionally seeking to find a way to behave by regulating himself.

The solution comes in realizing that a student's activity is a regulatory issue when he is seeking movement for regulation. With this understanding, the teacher could lovingly approach Billy and they could work out a way for Billy to have "elevator time" when he needed it. A schedule could be set up that worked with the teacher's schedule or Billy could be given the chance to express his need to regulate when he became dysregulated in the classroom.

Sound. Music can be exceptionally calming and it has been shown to actually change a person's brain wave patterns. In the womb, the fetus is constantly surrounded by the organizing rhythm and vibration of the heart. The brainstem is getting patterned at a very early age. Thus, it is not surprising that studies on classical music and Native American drumming have shown them to be effective forms of stress reduction. White noise machines and water fountains can also be used to provide comforting background noises.

Animals. Animals have a calming effect on human beings. Have you ever been to a psychotherapist's office and not seen a fish tank? Research has shown that watching fish randomly swim around in a tank can significantly decrease stress levels and lower blood pressure. Other animals that are soft and cuddly, such as hamsters and guinea pigs, can help create a calming atmosphere for children.

> **SURVEY SAYS:**
> _____
>
> "We had a class pet named Bunny Foo Foo I liked."

Breaks. Some children need to take frequent breaks and leave the classroom. Having library passes available to students can offer them these much-needed breaks. Granted, Billy is streetwise and will attempt to overuse this luxury of leaving the classroom, even when he is regulated. Boundaries and limitations will need to be held for such a tool to be used effectively instead of abused.

Simplicity. Decrease wall and ceiling decorations. Many classrooms have so many papers and posters stapled, hung, and pasted to walls and ceilings that even regulated students like Andy get overwhelmed. If you were to walk into a day spa, what do you notice about the environment? There is soft music, the walls are painted in a soft warm color, and there is a fountain of water creating a calming background sound. Consider how the décor of the classroom environment is influencing the regulation of the students.

> **SURVEY SAYS:**
> _____
>
> "I was very distracted. I used the bathroom as an excuse."

Lighting. Consider changing

and warming the lighting in the classroom. Stress and anxiety can increase when working with intense lighting, especially in rooms where fluorescent lighting is used. Using lamps with incandescent bulbs can aid in this as well as letting in as much possible natural light.

Food and Water. Keeping students regulated at the physical level is important to their ability to stay calm and focused, especially the Billys in the classroom, with experiences of neglect and not having enough food in the past. Their bodies can easily go into survival when they become hungry, which elicits the fear that they will never be fed again (there is that black-and-white thinking showing up again for Billy). Even for Andy, having the flexibility to have a snack and enough water can be beneficial to his overall demeanor. Keeping snacks and water available is ideal for helping to keep students regulated.

SURVEY SAYS:

"Kids should be able to eat their snacks whenever they want, as long as they don't bother anybody."

Safety. Sometimes, even when every measure has been taken to create a classroom of regulation, Billy may still not be able to maintain safety, thus becoming aggressive and violent. When Billy gets to this point, safety should always become the number one concern. Traditionally, when Billy exhibited these types of unsafe behaviors, he would be placed in a seclusion room and told he had to calm down before he could return to class. This type of response to Billy's aggression only escalates his survival mode, especially if he has had a trauma history of being left by himself. For a child like this, a seclusion room is the absolute worst solution for him.

SURVEY SAYS:

"No. I didn't like school because of the padded quiet room that made me so scared that I wet my pants and they made me clean it up with bleach and towels from the bathroom. They didn't let me change my clothes or wash my hands. I go to a different school now."

Secluding a child who does not have a sufficient regulatory system to calm down by himself is counterproductive and should never be an option. He will not be able to calm down on his own and it will be a traumatizing experience as he sinks deeper into a fight-or-flight response. It is like leaving a crying baby in a crib and expecting the baby to calm down on his own. The baby will only cry louder until he gets to a point where he has to shut down in order to stop the dangerous level of stress hormones being excreted. He stops crying out of survival, not out of regulation.

Instead, safety can be created by moving Billy into a safe room—a different room from the isolation room if he had negative experiences there—but a regulated and trusting adult needs to be with him. If the adult is in a loving place, free of control and fear, Billy will not have a need to attack. When the adult is not feeding more fear into Billy and adding a calm and loving presence, Billy's need to attack will decrease. This is where safety mantras that have been practiced and rehearsed can be exceptionally effective in getting Billy back to a place of rational thinking. Situations like this are even more quickly de-escalated when the adult with Billy in the containment area is someone he knows, trusts, and with whom he has past positive experiences.

Develop Relationship. If you reflect back onto your academic career from kindergarten to high school, who was your favorite teacher? Most of us can easily come up with an answer to this question. Yet the important point follows right behind: Why? Why was this your favorite teacher? Most likely, it was not because this teacher was well organized and gave good lectures. It was most likely due to this teacher's approachability and interest in you as not just a student, but as a person.

Out of everything listed in this chapter for motivating students, the most effective "tool" is relationship. Never underestimate the power of the relationship in the academic environment. It is the great motivator of all time. Unfortunately, many of our

> **SURVEY SAYS:**
>
> "Yes—I liked school because my teacher was nice she was always there to help me. And when I was struggling and would get mad she never gave up on me."

educational approaches to teaching students in the classroom are relationally disconnected experiences.

The teacher-student relationship addresses two of the most primary fears that every human on this planet has:

1. I'm not enough.
2. I won't be loved.

Children, however, are developmentally programmed to need relationship in order to curb these two great fears, more than adults. When a child goes through family experiences that fail to do this and conversely exasperate these fears, the result is a student who lives and breathes every moment out of these fears. With this intensity of fear occupying the mind, there is little room for clear, focused, and complex thinking.

When you have a strong relationship with someone, there is an inherent desire to please the other person. If your spouse or partner is upset with you, do you think he/she will stop off on the way home to buy you flowers or that special treat? No. Yet if this same person is floating on air in love with you, would the answer be different? Of course it would. As such, the teacher-student relationship is the key to awakening a student's internal drive.

> ### SURVEY SAYS:
>
> ---
>
> "Yes—I liked school this past year. I liked my teachers alot better this year because they understood me."

If you want to increase academic achievement, increase relationship. The two are directly correlated. Children like Billy need to be provided patterned, repetitive, relational experiences.

Enhancing the teacher-student relationship can be done in several small ways, many of which take very little extra time:

- Leave a note on the student's desk.
- Touch students more.
- Give students understanding and empathy.
- Listen to them; give them a voice.

- Scaffold them up with support and the resources they need.
- Give each student personal attention (greetings, short talks, compliments, acknowledgments, smiles, friendly eye contact).
- Express an attitude of "I care about you as a person."

Be willing to be vulnerable. Share some information about yourself (appropriate information) to show that you too are human and are willing to be exposed. It does not take a clinical degree in psychology to be able to relate to a student. It simply takes attention, awareness, and the willingness to take an interest in the student's perspective.

It is also important for children to have relational continuity, especially children with erratic histories of broken relationships. Switching teachers during the year can be disastrous for Billy. While "life happens" and this cannot always be prevented, helping a student rebuild a new relationship with a new teacher will be critical to the success of such a monumental change, as can be seen in the following example:

Billy was doing fairly well in third grade until about February. While there were several other factors that could have triggered him, such as the beginning of state testing or the anniversary of his adoptive placement, the one variable that stood out the most was the change in his primary classroom teacher. His teacher, one he adored and favored, was suddenly replaced due to an emergency within her family. By the beginning of March, Billy's behaviors had intensified and it seemed as if he had completely regressed back to the beginning of the school year. The switch over in teachers was addressed only minimally at a class level, and the students were expected to move forward as if everything was the same. Billy's parents went to the new teacher and explained how Billy was missing the previous teacher and had not yet had a chance to develop a strong relationship with the new teacher. Arrangements were made for the new teacher to meet Billy at the park that following Saturday so they could have one-on-one time. Billy also began coming to class ten minutes early each day prior to the first bell. During

the morning time with the teacher, Billy was given jobs to
help the teacher, such as washing the whiteboard, along with
the chance to build a deeper, more meaningful relationship
with her. After only two weeks, Billy's behavior returned
back to where it had been prior to the change in teachers.

Never minimize the impact on students when teachers are changed during the school year or when students are moved to different classrooms midyear.

Involve Parental Support, Not Parental Fear. Teachers traditionally have used the parent-child relationship in a fear-based way to get children motivated. The teacher says to Billy:

"If you don't get your work done ...
"If you don't behave ...
"If you don't get focused and pay attention ...

... then I'm going to call your parents."

This threat of calling the parents is missing a grand opportunity to motivate children through the influence of a relationship rather than trying to motivate them through the threat of a relationship. The two are radically different.

For Andy, threatening to call his parents will typically work because he has a relationship with his parents. He cares about them and what they think about him. Deep down, Andy wants to please his parents, so he responds to this threat.

Billy, however, is still working to keep his parents at a distance in order to protect himself from the vulnerability of an intimate parent-child relationship. Threatening to call his parents actually helps him fuel his campaign against his parents. Disapproval from his parents will not elicit a positive response in Billy and, in fact, will sometimes work to drive Billy further away from his parents. This is why Billy may actually increase the intensity of his negative behaviors with such a threat.

In some cases, Billy is actually trying to get his parents' approval. In this case, a threat to call his parents would ignite his stress-response system. He is scared that if he does not win his parent's approval, he will lose his parents. Adopted and foster children live in a perpetual state of fear that their parents will simply give up on them and send them back at any moment of any day. Billy's underdeveloped ability to modulate stress will then manifest itself into more negative behaviors and he may spiral out of control. His ability to maintain any sense of regulation would be severely challenged.

Schools need to team up together with parents to help regulate Billy. When Billy gets upset and the teacher is unable to help regulate Billy's stress response system, the teacher can suggest that Billy call his mom or dad. Taking two or three minutes for Billy to connect by phone can be just enough to help him get back on track.

For many students, a daily phone call to a parent as a proactive measure can be a powerful way to help them interrupt their stress patterns. Billy's system is not equipped to handle six hours in a school environment; his window of stress tolerance simply is not that large. Allowing him a break or two during these six hours gives him a chance to reregulate throughout the day before behavioral issues surface.

When possible, most adults check in with their significant other during the workday. In fact, if we do not check in, we might hear about it when we arrive home: "Why didn't you call me today?" It is a healthy coping mechanism to chunk our day into smaller pieces with relational breaks throughout.

Allowing phone calls to the parent is a developmentally sensitive approach to working with a child like Billy. When infants become toddlers, their mobility increases but their regulatory system is not yet fully developed. During this stage of development, they will wander away from their parents to explore their surroundings. These early exploratory experiences are limited, as the toddlers then run back to the parent to reconnect. They run to explore and then run back to reconnect and reregulate. This type of behavior is repetitive and gives the child a chance to be on his own to practice self-regulation, but then it immediately affords him the chance to reregulate back with the parent.

We need to re-create this type of coming and going for Billy. Giving him a chance to be on his own at school for a couple of hours, then allowing him to call or text a parent to get reregulated, is giving him practice to later becoming fully able to self-regulate. Eventually, Billy will not need this type of intermediate reconnection and will be able to make it through the whole school day.

Here is an account of a dad's interaction by phone with his ninth-grade "Billy" at school:

When Billy becomes upset, his sensory system gets revved up, and going to class becomes too difficult. The counselor called me the other day and said that Billy was refusing to go to class. While on the phone with me (and Billy knew I was on the phone), the counselor asked Billy again if he would like to return to class. I heard Billy reply, "No, I most certainly do not." I asked to speak to Billy to help him regulate back down and to connect with him and his struggle. The conversation went something like this:

> *Dad:*   "What's going on, buddy?"
> *Billy:* "I have a headache and it is piercing my brain so I'm not going to go to class and deliberately put myself in more pain."
> *Dad:*   "I'm so sorry to hear that."
> *Billy:* "Nobody can stop me from sitting here all day."
> *Dad:*   "You're right."

At this point, we sat in silence. It was not a "You're in trouble" silence but an "I'm here just to love you" silence. After a bit, I continued:

> *Dad:*   "Is there anything I can do for you now?"
> *Billy:* "I could ask you to come pick me up but I know you won't."

Billy knows my "General Patton" stance that he will need to learn how to manage in school and I will not be coming to get him unless it is an absolute emergency. We ended the conversation without me trying to take control over him but encouraging him to regulate and return to class. He, however, did not go back to class and sat in the counselor's office the rest of the day. When he got home, he got on his bike and took a good thirty-minute ride. Most parents would not have allowed this, as a consequence, but I know Billy. He needed time to get this out of his system and process. The next morning I went to wake him up and he said to me:

> Billy: *"I told you. I'm never going back to school."*
>
> Dad: *"I understand it is hard. But remember the deal is that you need to go. Staying home is not an option."*

Billy got ready for school without another word of resistance and had no trouble making it through the entire day. I know that by giving him the support, holding the needed boundaries, and not trying to force or control him is what he needed to uncover the natural internal motivation that is inside of him. He has been having a wonderful school year thus far and has not refused to go to any classes since this incident.

CHAPTER EIGHT

Transitioning

■

Change has a considerable psychological impact on the human mind. To the fearful it is threatening because it means that things may get worse. To the hopeful it is encouraging because things may get better. To the confident it is inspiring because the challenge exists to make things better.

~ King Whitney, Jr.

T he word "transition" is defined as the "passage from one form, state, style, or place to another."[1] It is the movement from point A to point B. When it comes to children, we naturally support, nurture, and protect them when they have to make transitions. "Sally, hold my hand when we cross this street." "Johnny, hold onto the cart as we move through the store."

Adults hold the responsibility for protecting and teaching children how to navigate the art of transitioning successfully. Yet this adult protective system can fail to sustain children because some transitions that children face are far greater than what their underdeveloped nervous systems can handle. As a result, we have children who experience transitional trauma early in their lives. A child being adopted out of an international orphanage is taken from the familiar to the completely unfamiliar with adults he does not know. A foster child is moved from one foster home to another with adults he deems "untrustable." A child who undergoes multiple painful medical procedures in various hospitals in multiple departments with multiple doctors has no control over what is being done to him.

Such events have a significant impact on a child's level of fear response to transitional experiences later on in life. The impact can manifest during both major and minor transitional experiences. The type or magnitude of the transition itself is not the issue; the issue is the fear of actually making a transition. Our brains rely on history to determine the safety of the present. Billy's past experiences of change were negative and hurtful, therefore any and all future experiences of change will be negative and hurtful.

Traditional View

Traditionally, children are expected to do what adults tell them to do, with minimal resistance or defiance. While this concept is usually reasonable, it negates that children with transitional trauma in their histories cannot simply do what they are told.

Children like Andy have had protection, security, and support around the transitions in their lives. This makes following adult instructions and directives easier. Andy has no reason to believe he will not be safe; such a thought is vacant from his mindset.

When a child like Billy refuses to get up and go to school or becomes disruptive when it is time to move from the classroom to his music class, he has been viewed as defiant or lazy. The traditional interpretation has been outcome focused. Movement from point A to point B has been the goal, with a lack of consideration as to why one child, Andy, is able to accomplish this while another child, Billy, is not.

Major transitions within schools are recognized as being difficult for every child, including Andy, because they represent milestone moments. Such transitions include back-to-school time, movement from elementary school to middle school, and graduation from high school to "the real world." While these events should be acknowledged as difficult times for students, less obvious transitional times also need to be acknowledged.

Classroom Management. When smaller and less significant events are acknowledged, they have traditionally been viewed in the framework of classroom management. The term "classroom management" speaks to the idea of controlling the group's behavior as one singular unit. Transitioning has been seen as an issue from the group perspective, with little consideration to the needs of the individual students. This approach works for a classroom of Andys. Yet when a child like Billy is given this approach, his nervous system does not respond in the same manner.

One management technique traditionally recommended to help children make transitions uses "attention grabbers." Attention grabbers are designed to "grab" the students' attention and direct them through the next steps. Hand clapping, whistling, and flickering of the lights are popular methods. However, these sensory signals can actually worsen transitions for children with trauma. Because trauma often overloads the nervous system, intense sensory stimulation cannot be processed effectively. The result is that Billy's already sensitive nervous system becomes overloaded with these attention grabbers and he demonstrates this overload through negative behaviors.

Time warnings have traditionally been used to give children time to prepare for impending transitions. However, many children with trauma histories have a limited sense of time and are impaired in their ability to think sequentially, organize, and process their thoughts. For example, if the teacher instructs the class to clean up and gives them five minutes to do so, Billy faces two deficiencies. First, he has no understanding as to how long five minutes is; it is too nebulous a concept from his concrete framework and he cannot conceptualize it. Second, Billy's disorganized thinking cannot comprehend on its own what needs to be done in order to "clean up."

Billy is expected to think like Andy, and older Billys especially are expected to know the developmental tasks that are typically accomplished by his age. The result is a frustrated teacher and a painful misunderstanding of Billy. ("It works with the other children, so it must be that Billy isn't listening or respecting the rules.") Billy then receives punishment for a task he is not able to perform rather than a task he is not willing to perform.

New View

In the normal course of a child's development, he experiences biological, psychological, and emotional changes as he grows from infancy to adulthood. The child progresses from a state of dependency to autonomy. When a child like Andy grows up in an optimal environment, he has the opportunity to master each developmental milestone in sequence and in completion. His ability to self-regulate and adjust to the uncertainties of the world equips him for the demands of the school environment.

When a child's life becomes interrupted through traumatic life experiences, his normal course of development becomes fractured and incomplete. The result is a child who is exceptionally sensitive to uncertainty and change. Pain happened for Billy when his life was disrupted; pain happened when change happened. This pattern sets Billy's program for how he handles (or does not handle) change now and in the future.

In the school environment this equates to one word: transitioning. Billy is going to be challenged moving from point A to point B. Trauma causes black-and-white thinking. So for Billy, all change equals pain, no matter how small or minute the change may be. Change can be as simple as moving from one classroom to another, going from the classroom to specials, coming into the classroom at the start of the day, switching from a math worksheet to a science assignment, or exiting the cafeteria and returning back to class. In Billy's mind, though, these are not simple changes because any change will bring about disaster.

> **SURVEY SAYS:**
> _____
> "Keep things the same on set days."

Instead of regarding Billy as bad or disruptive during transitions, it must be understood that Billy is sensitive to change and needs help to learn that change can be safe. Taking points off his point chart will not correct his behavior—it will only reinforce his fear of transitioning.

Billy needs support, understanding, and connection during transitional times to reprogram his system. As he is able to experience positive times of transitions, he will learn how to make these transitions on his own. Asking him to be as capable as Andy at the present time will only distance him further from healing and change.

Remember, trauma often overloads the normal capacity of the body's nervous system. To work the body out of this overwhelm, it takes slowly and methodically moving toward regulation, back into a state of calm. For instance, if someone has hypothermia, the process of rewarming the body is slow and methodical. Increasing the body's core temperature too quickly in this state would cause serious and permanent damage or even death. For our children who live in a sensitive, hyper- or hypo-aroused state induced by past trauma, they too need help and support at a slow pace to move out of it. In trauma healing, it is known as "titration,"[2] a process of taking small steps to allow the nervous system to stabilize and return to a more natural state of calm arousal.

In the school environment, the Billys need the same approach. Anything too abrupt, challenging, or strenuous will be counterproductive. They need support around change, and they need to be scaffolded up until they can learn to do it on their own.

There are several key transitional times that should be addressed for Billy. These include changing classrooms and subjects, cafeteria time, recess, field trips, before and after school, beginning of the school year, ending of the school year, holiday breaks, and graduation from high school. Providing strong structure, routine, and predictability during these times will provide the external stability that he is missing internally.

Changing Classrooms and Subjects. Moving from one classroom to another and switching from one subject to another are two classic examples of transitioning in the school setting. For elementary school children, changing classrooms is typically moving from the classroom to a special like art, music, or physical education. For middle schoolers and high schoolers, this equates to switching to six different classrooms each day through crowded and loud hallways.

In elementary school, the transition from one classroom to another is typically orderly and controlled by the teachers. Lining up in a single file line does provide regulation, and for children like Andy these transitions are not an issue. However, children like Billy, who view any transition as a

SURVEY SAYS:

"I always got in trouble in line because kids bothered me."

threat, will typically struggle and act out negatively when making this transition. Their histories of getting hurt or being overwhelmed during a transition have set the blueprint for how movement will be viewed for all present and future occasions.

Trauma keeps the brain in a simplified framework. Billy is not sophisticated enough to distinguish one transition as "good" and another as "bad." Concrete thinking prevails: All transitions are bad. Panic will be the first response until a level of healing can happen. Therefore, it is in Billy's best interest to learn how to develop the flexibility to be able to handle these transitions. Several suggestions follow.

Greet Each Student. Connecting in relationship with every student is one of the most effective ways to help students successfully make transitions. Whether it is the start of the morning or a return to the classroom, each time the student arrives back into the classroom, he should be greeted. The message conveyed to the student is: "You are important and special to this class. Welcome back. You are in a safe and familiar place and I'm here to keep you safe."

Calling each student by name can also send the message that he is unique and an important part of the family classroom. "Good morning, Billy" is much more penetrative than "Good morning." As Dale Carnegie said, "Remember that a person's name is to that person the sweetest and most important sound in any language."[3]

Prepare. Prepare students ahead of time for the transition. Watch the clock and stop all work and instructions two minutes prior to the bell ringing. Too many times these final two minutes are jam-packed with last-minute instructions and assignments that only serve to arouse Billy's nervous system, setting him up for failure before the transition even begins. During these two minutes, create an atmosphere of calm:

SURVEY SAYS:

"Have teachers and other people at school greet us in the morning, like they are happy to see us."

- Lower the lights.
- Lead the students in some deep breathing.
- Sing a song (for the elementary students).
- Play a soothing song (or part of a song) every time before the bell rings so it becomes a signal for the body to automatically relax.
- Remind the students verbally how important they are to you (no matter how the class behaved that day).

> **SURVEY SAYS:**
>
> "[I] feel better when my teacher is there with me."

Provide Assistance. Providing assistance can decrease a student's level of overwhelm. Have Billy either in the front of the line near an adult or in the back of the line near an adult. Billy may feel safer in the back of the line because then he can see everybody, which minimizes the surprise factor of someone coming up behind him and hurting him. If it were a middle school or high school student, having Billy walk with a teacher to the next class through the crowded and noisy hallway would be an ideal solution. However, the social implications of this could be devastating. Pairing Billy up with Andy for safe peer support could provide the support Billy needs to decrease his overwhelm in the hallway, without the negative social implications.

> **SURVEY SAYS:**
>
> "Something else that would make me want to get up and go to school is that my friends are there to back me up if I need help with something."

Use Music and Songs. Music works to calm the right brain, the area of the brain most sensitive to stress. Songs for transitioning children can be effective in helping them embrace the change. One of Barney's (the famous purple dinosaur) all-time most popular songs is "Clean Up." Singing a song such as this as a whole class can help Billy feel supported while also building his level of security by calming down his brain. A wonderful resource with an extensive listing of songs for every type of transition in a school is "Songs for Teaching:

Using Music to Promote Learning" (www.songsforteaching.com/transitions.htm).

Cafeteria Time. Studies have shown that the sound level in some American school cafeterias measures up to 85 decibels.[4] This is equivalent to the noise of a lawnmower. Sitting in a school cafeteria for twenty minutes with this type of noise will tax a child's ability to regulate and integrate such an overload of sensory input, even for a child like Andy.

Andy's system is flexible, which equips him to be able to leave the cafeteria and settle his system back down upon returning to the classroom.

Andy enters the classroom slightly aroused but still able to sit down and focus on the next task at hand. Billy's nervous system does not have this capability. Billy arrives back into the classroom and his system continues to be operating on "high," as if he is still in the cafeteria. The solution is to help Billy adjust through supportive and proactive measures:

- The teacher eats with the class during lunch and sits next to Billy to help regulate him. Though this is typically the teacher's time to have down time, many teachers prefer this option because it ensures an easier afternoon, so the investment of energy and loss of free time is well worth it.

- Before leaving the cafeteria, the teacher instructs the class to take two deep breaths together prior to returning to the classroom.

- In the lineup back to the classroom, Billy is at the front of the line with the teacher, or a teacher's aide stands next to Billy. The aide or the teacher checks in with Billy with a quick "Hi Billy. We're going back to the classroom now. How are you doing?"

- Leave the classroom lights on a dim setting so when the students walk into the class, the room provides a calming environment. The teacher instructs the students to take two more deep breaths and slowly turns up the lights when the stress level in the students appears to be returning to a normal level.

- If the cafeteria still proves too much for Billy, even with the above measures, give Billy an alternative place to eat lunch. Select a quiet place (such as the library or the counselor's office) and have Billy eat lunch with an adult he trusts. This one-on-one time could be exactly what Billy needs, providing him with enough regulation to handle the rest of the school afternoon.

Recess. For some children, play and social time can be as stressful as academics, especially when it involves recess. A playground is a large open area with many children playing at the same time in a multitude of activities, with minimal supervision. This is the epitome of unpredictability. Children like Billy are left to their own devices (which are underdeveloped and immature) to navigate this environment. They do not know what to expect, do not feel safe, and have most likely had negative playground experiences that keep them locked into a negative perception of this environment.

Ironically, though, it is most likely the child like Billy who absolutely needs recess to "blow off steam." So now we have a child who needs recess yet gets completely overwhelmed by recess. With enough supervision in the playground (with a regulated adult) sandwiched before and after with transitional help, success is possible. Some schools have assigned a "recess coach" to help monitor and structure this time for students. Here are some ideas for providing transitional help around recess time:

- Before recess, the teacher makes certain that Billy understands where the class is heading and on how they are going to get there.

- Billy, along with the entire class, is made aware of what is going to happen once the class returns from recess. Even if the routine is the same one the class has followed for three months, the information is still provided to give Billy predictability.

- Billy is given options as to what to do in the event that he gets overwhelmed on the playground. Instead of feeling powerless or helpless (and acting out), he is given ways to get resourced. This may be with a safe and emotionally connected adult on the playground, giving him a break to get some water and take some deep breaths, or choosing an activity that physically regulates his body, like swinging.

- Billy may need a smaller area in which to play. Sectioning off a small area of the playground to create more physical containment will decrease his overwhelm. This space can incrementally be enlarged once he feels safer.

- Once Billy is on the playground, an adult can help him slowly transition into play, interacting with Billy and helping him adjust to the change in the environment. Typically, once children hit the playground, they run and disperse like a heard of wild horses. This is too abrupt for Billy; if he is given more transitional time with an adult helping him get settled into an activity like jumping rope or riding on the merry-go-round, he has more chance for a positive experience.

- When it is time to clean up and put away the balls and other pieces of recreational equipment, Billy may not understand what this completely entails. When the teacher says, "In five minutes we need to line up. Make sure you're doing what it takes now so you're ready when I blow the whistle," Billy's mind cannot comprehend what it means to "get ready." He may need an adult to walk him through this process step-by-step. This will teach him through experience how to eventually get ready on his own.

- When given the choice between going to recess or to a quiet environment like the library, some children actually choose the library. The library is calm, quiet, and safe. Despite the benefits of physical exercise, some children require more down time instead of play time for their nervous system to recover from the challenges of the morning, equipping them to rejuvenate themselves for the afternoon.

Field Trips. It is very common for a child like Billy to become more disruptive the day before a field trip. The teacher will typically respond to him in a threatening and punitive manner: "Billy, if you don't behave, you're not going to be able to go on the field trip tomorrow."

The reality is that it is the field trip that has stirred up Billy's anxiety. Either the fear of going to a new place and changing his routine or the sheer excitement of the field trip could be dysregulating him. He then feels more threatened by the teacher's fear-based and punitive statement, so he continues to react negatively. He does not have the capacity to switch to a calm state and become compliant. When Billy is not allowed to go on the trip and stays at school the next day, exactly what he needed has ironically taken place. Billy created the safety plan he was seeking—he was communicating that the field trip was too much. It is a brilliant strategy for a child who was not offered the regulatory help he needed to manage the field trip.

The differences between Andy's and Billy's perceptions of the field trip need to be recognized. Andy is excited about the field trip; Billy is scared about the field trip. Andy has a relatively well-developed regulatory system to maintain self-control with this level of excitement; Billy does not.

In prepping for field trips, traditional resources give teachers recommendations on how to plan the logistics. These recommendations discuss how to prepare students from an academic perspective and offer ways to integrate the field trip experience upon returning to school. These recommendations, however, fail to acknowledge the emotional prepping students may need. Billy's ability to navigate and handle a field trip successfully would greatly increase if the teacher were to implement the following strategies:

- Acknowledge the spectrum of feelings (excitement to fear) that may come up when discussing the field trip. This could be done on a whole-class basis or individually with Billy.

- Show pictures of the place the class will be visiting, with emphasis on "what you will see" and "what to expect." The goal of this exercise is to decrease the unknown for Billy.

- Give a detailed schedule of how the day will unfold. Billy needs to know what is going to happen "next." It is important that this plan be followed as closely as possible. Due to the nature of field trips, plans may change; if they do, the teacher should acknowledge the change to both Billy and the class and help the students process it. Instead of simply expecting Billy to "go with the flow," the teacher must recognize that Billy lacks this kind of emotional flexibility. He lives in a rigid world internally because that is what creates safety, so when the world expects him to be spontaneous and flexible, his behavior will demonstrate this Grand Canyon–sized gap.

- Suggest to the parent that Billy's family visit the place where the field trip will be prior to the class trip. If Billy can visit this new environment within the safety of his family system, it can decrease his fear when in the context of a large number of students.

- Ask Billy's parent to chaperone the field trip to give him an adult he trusts and who he can regulate off of during the experience. If the parent is unable to attend, have an adult with whom Billy is familiar (such as the teacher) be his group leader.

- Keep Billy in a smaller group of students so the adult-to-student ratio is low.

- Check in with Billy throughout the trip to help him stay regulated. Stay connected with him at an emotional level.

- Have a back-up plan in case all of the previously mentioned strategies are not enough to keep Billy from getting too overwhelmed during the trip. Never threaten to send him home during the field trip; rather, offer him the choice of having his parent pick him up in the event that he becomes overwhelmed. When he feels like he has an escape hatch instead of feeling trapped, he has a greater chance of feeling safe enough to make it through the entire day.

- If Billy is showing an increased level of fear the day before, give him the option of either staying at school or going on the trip. He may not be ready to go, and children have a good sense if something is going to be too overwhelming for them. Many children actually choose to stay at school when it is not used as a punishment or threat. It may be exactly what they need, and this gives them time to heal in order to make the next field trip a successful experience.

Before and After School. One of the most stressful times in a student's day can be before and/or after school. In the mornings, when children arrive at school prior to the first bell, they are typically all placed together in an open and unstructured environment such as a courtyard. The synergy of all the students together, emitting anxiety about the start of the school day combined with the stress of the social dynamics among them, is intense. Just ten minutes in this type of environment can exhaust Billy's entire window of stress tolerance. The result is that when he walks into his first class, after his nervous system is shocked by the ringing of the bell, he is moments if not seconds away from his breaking point. He has no internal space to even begin the day with the strenuous demands of academics.

After-school containment areas can also be distressing for Billy. By the end of the school day, even the Andys of the school are stressed out. At this point, we have an entire school body that is physically tired, mentally stretched, and socially anxious. Teachers and paraprofessionals as well reflect this state; they have been in the classroom working hard to regulate and maintain structure for the students. Mix all these dynamics into a school cafeteria, auditorium, or playground for an Extended Day program and you have a recipe for failure.

Drive Billy to School. The ideal solution would be for Billy to completely avoid unstructured environments before school. They are simply too much for him. Instead, Billy's parent should drive him to school and wait in the car with Billy just before the first bell rings. The time spent in the parked car is an excellent time to help regulate and transition Billy into his school day. Conversations about what is going on at school for the day (such as tests, topics being studied, and social situations) can be opened up by the parent. Or perhaps, quiet-down time is what Billy needs at this point with the parent. Either way, Billy would be given the time to prepare himself for the next six hours of challenge.

Walk Billy to Class. If the child is younger, the parent should arrange with the teacher to walk Billy directly to the classroom about ten minutes before the first bell. The parent is then directly able to help Billy change from one regulated adult to another. This "changing of the guard," without the other students in the classroom, eliminates most of the morning stress. The teacher can assign Billy tasks to be a helper, like sharpening pencils, erasing the white board, and passing out papers. This gives Billy a chance to build his relationship with the teacher as well as develop a greater sense of purpose and self-esteem. Additionally, once the first bell rings, Billy is already in the classroom and settled as the other students arrive.

Find Alternatives to the Courtyard. If Billy absolutely has to arrive early to school or needs to stay after school due to the parent's work schedule, find an alternative location for Billy. The library can be an excellent calming environment for him. For many children, books are a great regulatory tool. When Billy is told he will be going to the library instead of the courtyard, the delivery is key. Instead of saying to Billy, "You can't stay in the courtyard anymore because you don't know how to behave," the delivery's focus should be relationship based with a concern for his well-being: "Billy, we have arranged for you to go visit Ms. Jones in the library every morning before school so you'll feel safer and be able to stay calm with books before classes begin."

Stay with a Regulated Adult. If all of the above measures are not possible and Billy has to be in the large-group setting before or after school, choose the most regulated adult supervising the area to watch over Billy. Have Billy stay close by this person, even holding hands with her if Billy is on the younger end of the spectrum, in order to help Billy sustain himself in this overstimulating environment. This individual's focus is not punitive in nature but relationship-based to essentially wrap Billy with emotional and physical safety.

Beginning of the School Year. Many parents would agree that the beginning of the new school year is one of the most stressful times of the entire year for their children. Children who were doing well over the summer break suddenly begin to become anxious and regress to their old negative and disruptive behaviors once the new school year approaches. Conversely, parents are ready to do the happy dance because summer vacation is over and they are more than ready for their children to return to school. It is a difficult mix with two opposing agendas.

Even when Billy is returning to his same school, the fear of the unknown is still going to be a challenge. The "new" factor is still high: new classroom, new teacher, new students, new friends, new subjects, new rules, new expectations, new backpack, new shoes, new notebooks, new pencils, new lunchbox. Everything new is, well, new. And new is unfamiliar. Even new things that are fun, like new clothes and a new backpack, do not fit into the category of familiar, thus they add an element of stress.

Meet the Teacher Before "Meet the Teacher." Billy needs to become acquainted with his new teacher(s) prior to the start of the first day, even prior to the "Meet the Teacher" event at the school. This event is typically an anxiety-driven event due to the high levels of excitement and anticipation brought about by the students attending. Andy benefits from this event. Billy decompensates from this event.

Some teachers have made home visits to students like Billy so that the initial introduction is made within the safety of the students' own home. If this is not possible, Billy should come to the school and meet his teacher during the week before the start of school, during the teacher's planning week. While this time is typically the teacher's time to prepare for the new school year, if the teacher can invest fifteen minutes to meet with Billy, the benefits will be immense. The more the teacher can invest in developing a relationship prior to day one of school, the more Billy has time to feel safe and the more the new school year becomes familiar and safe for him.

> ### SURVEY SAYS:
>
> ---
>
> "Yes [I liked school]. Because it's a new school and they are helping me and I have some new friends. And the principal is nice."

Meet More Than the Teacher. Think beyond the teacher. It is important for Billy to meet other school personnel in order to give him a chance to develop connections and relationships outside of his immediate class(es). Introduce Billy to the cafeteria staff, the janitor, the receptionist, the librarian, and anyone else he might see during a typical day. Set up a lunch date with the principal. Instead of the principal being someone to fear, flip this around and help Billy create a relationship with the person who is in the top position at the school, which conversely can offer one of the most secure relationships for Billy.

Tour the School. When attending a new school, Billy needs to become familiar with the entire school campus. This includes the cafeteria, the school counselor's office, the principal's office, the library, and the restrooms. Knowing only where his classes are will not provide the level of security he needs. If Billy can be given a visual map, along with a complete tour of his surroundings, he can become better grounded and physically more secure.

End of the School Year. The entire energy of a classroom can shift beginning as early as a month before school ends for summer vacation. The level of structure tends to decrease in the classroom, a restlessness can set in after a rigorous academic year for both the students and the teachers (especially after state testing in public schools), and the weather begins to change so it becomes more inviting to be outdoors than indoors. Additionally, children like Billy, with a history of broken and lost relationships, can become anxious about losing their teacher. For example, one mom relayed that her fourth grader expressed to his teacher that he wanted to fail so he could have her again the next year.

Address the issues of this transition directly with Billy and with the entire class, with a focus on the feelings associated with this change. The expression of the feelings can work to head off the fallout of negative behaviors. Ignoring the rise in unsettling feelings associated with the change from school to summer can lead to a difficult and unpleasant end of what might have been a very successful school year.

Help Billy make the transition from being with a teacher five days a week, six hours a day, to having zero contact. This change is too abrupt for his nervous system as well as for his psyche. He needs a step-down approach to shifting out of this relationship. If the teacher and parent can work together, set up ways for Billy and his teacher to communicate (email, letters, or phone calls) once school is out for the summer. Slowly move Billy out of this relationship instead of expecting him to go through an abrupt withdrawal, which will ultimately result in negative behaviors.

Holiday Breaks. Whether it is a one-day break from school or a two-week break during the holiday season, such breaks are an interruption to Billy's normal, predictable, structured, and safe routine. Transitioning into the break and then out of the break can be beyond difficult for everyone involved: Billy, teachers, and parents. A rise in Billy's negative behaviors is typically the fallout of what is supposed to be a fun, relaxing, and revitalizing time.

Because these breaks are preplanned on the school calendar, it is entirely possible to prepare Billy for them ahead of time. Create a countdown for the number of days until the break, so Billy can visually see the number of days until he has a holiday break. Make a paper chain with him as a way to tangibly count down each day. On the reverse, once Billy is home, count down the days until he goes back to school. The more Billy has an understanding of what will be happening next and how many days until his schedule will change or return to the normal routine, the better he can handle these transitions.

During the breaks at home, create a visual schedule of how the day will unfold for Billy. He has to know what will come next, otherwise he may assume that what will come next will be something bad. Billy's level of anxiety during such breaks can be greatly decreased when he has input into what will be on the family agenda and when he has a visual awareness of it. Taking the time and making the effort to give Billy this information will save the parent from the same maddening question every two minutes throughout an entire day: "What are we doing next?" "What are we doing next?" "What are we doing next?" "What are we doing next?" "What are we doing next?"

Graduation from High School. When Billy reaches high school, he may actually be doing well and succeeding—until his senior year. All of a sudden, Billy goes from making A's and B's to D's and F's. Instead of just assuming Billy is a typical senior experiencing senioritis, this drastic change in grades begs the number one question we must ask of any child's behavior: "What is driving this behavior?"

This type of failing behavior along with the timing of Billy's scheduled graduation is no coincidence. It is actually a foolproof plan of Billy's. If Billy fails his senior year, he has one more year to attend high school. This equates to not having to enter into the "real world."

Billy avoids having to change environments and he grants himself one more year of familiarity at school. The unknown is now further off in the distance. Additionally, he affords himself one more year of childhood. Billy guarantees himself one more year of living at home where he is provided shelter, transportation, food, and the basic living essentials. This, in fact, is a brilliant plan (from Billy's perspective)! For Billy, even the thought of being out of a structured, predictable, and familiar environment is not only frightening, it is terrifying—yes, terrifying.

One of the biggest issues Billy deals with at this point in his life is the impending loss of childhood. By graduating, he is officially an adult. The chance of going back and re-creating his senior year, claiming for himself what Andy was afforded, however magical this thinking might be, is about to be thwarted. A powerful resistance to stepping into his future and into adulthood dominates his every move at this point in his development. No amount of coaxing, no consequence implemented, and no punishment delivered holds as much weight as the loss of his childhood. Thus, traditional attempts at changing his behavior or disciplining him will be futile.

Billy's fears need to be brought to the surface. In the context of a safe relationship, he must be given the opportunity to voice his fears. Billy's thinking stems from the emotional part of the brain, the limbic system. All logic and reasoning will be met with resistance and defensiveness. The response he receives from the listener, therefore, cannot be that of why he needs to graduate, how he is about to be an adult, and why he cannot live at home as a freeloader.

Giving Billy a chance to have a voice and be received with understanding, compassion, tolerance, kindness, openness, and acceptance allows him a chance to bring these fears to the surface instead of letting them drive his every move. Once Billy can express his fears and be heard, he has a greater ability to empower himself with solutions and be willing to listen to others' solutions.

Billy's transition out of the home needs to be at a slower pace than Andy's. His parents should work with Billy's school counselor, along with Billy, to develop a plan for Billy following graduation. This might include Billy living at home, attending a community college or technical school, and working at a low-stress job or volunteering. When Billy has a clearer picture of what life will entail following high school, his fears will decrease and so too will the sabotaging of his senior year.

Parents need to redefine their age of adulthood for Billy. Billy might be eighteen years old chronologically, but he is much younger emotionally and developmentally. Hence, he will not yet be ready to live on his own with all the responsibilities and demands this requires. This does not mean he needs to live at home with no responsibilities but rather with a plan to help him become equipped to eventually live on his own.

Healing takes time and patience. Small steps lead to larger steps. *Titration ... titration ... titration.* Trust in the process and once the fear is removed for Billy, he will be able to make this move toward adulthood more gracefully, without as much negativity and resistance.

CHAPTER NINE

Teachers

■

We cannot hold a torch to light another's
path without brightening our own.
~ Ben Sweetland

D ictionaries define a teacher simply as "a person who teaches or instructs others."[1] Unfortunately, this definition dehumanizes the role of a teacher in a student's life. A robot could easily fit this definition of one who teaches or instructs others. In fact, log onto YouTube.com and you will find a plethora of videos that teach or instruct, with absolutely no face-to-face human interaction.

Technology can teach but it cannot relate. What teachers bring to the art of instructing, albeit more nebulous and harder to define, is relationship. The very definition of a teacher given above verges on being insulting to teachers, as it completely ignores the most valuable aspect of a teacher's effectiveness. The gift a teacher brings to her* students goes far beyond her ability to teach or instruct; it is her ability to build a nurturing, trusting, and compassionate relationship with her students. Therein lies the key to her effectiveness.

When students vote for "Teacher of the Year," how many teachers are given this accolade if they are disconnected from their students? None. When teachers are chosen for this award, it is primarily based on how they relate to their students, not solely on how well they teach. A Google search on the Internet gives a few typical examples of why teachers were nominated for Teacher of the Year:

- "Students love his class because he is able to build strong relationships with them."

* *Throughout this book, the teacher is referred to in the feminine in order to avoid clumsy construction.*

- "There is nothing she won't do for her students."
- "He has unending patience; he understands the needs of each student."
- "He has a rapport with the students that is unparalleled by any other teachers in the building while maintaining his position as an authority figure within his classroom."
- "She is enthusiastic and extremely supportive of everything her students want to try."

Traditional View

Traditionally, the teacher has been seen as the authority, the manager, the boss, and the "chief" in the classroom. While having a strong leader is certainly imperative, the teacher's role has been centered on being in charge through this position, supported by the hierarchy and dominance that comes with it. In essence, the teacher has been the "queen" of the classroom, ruling over her powerless and voiceless peasants in the kingdom.

This hierarchical structure creates an "us against them" mentality for teachers and students. The popular cliché for teachers, "Once you've yelled, you've lost the battle," exemplifies this. It implies that the classroom is a battlefield, where the teachers must prevail in order to maintain law and order.

> **SURVEY SAYS:**
>
> "[School would be better if] the teacher would walk around the class engaging with all the kids!"

Traditionally, teachers have been expected to run a classroom where academics are the focus, with little time or energy to spend on the students' emotional and social needs. Students are to sit in a standardized classroom, be standardized pegs that fit into standardized slots, and follow instructions and rules without questioning authority.

This cookie-cutter approach dehumanizes the classroom environment and ignores the incredible power of the teacher-student relationship. True "power" and "control" do not come through authority but through relational influence. Children inherently want to please those with whom they have a strong relationship. Ignoring this natural motivator has been a shameful loss in maintaining and improving the academic environment.

The reality, especially in the times we are living, is that the more students are controlled and not given a voice, the more we will have students misbehaving, rebelling, and

> **SURVEY SAYS:**
>
> "No seclusion rooms. When I feel angry it feels like everything is closing in on me. A big space helps me calm down more."

dropping out, particularly children like Billy. This type of traditional classroom ends up providing more time for Billy to spend in time-out, detention, or worse, in a seclusion room, areas of school that provide the least amount of academic instruction.

New View

Teachers are humans. Students are human. Merge these two vital forces and what comes to fruition is a powerful teacher-student relationship. This relationship far outweighs any other technique created by educators to further a student's academic achievement.

Humans as a species are designed to be in relationship and to be in community. Relationship is what defines humanity. When relationships are neglected or placed secondary to other goals, such as academics, both students and teachers suffer. Integrating this relational concept back into the classroom is the solution.

Redefining the Teacher-Student Relationship. The first priority in the classroom, even over learning, should be the teacher-student relationship. This relationship remains the focus at all times because relationships bring security for Billy. When Billy is given understanding, validation, tolerance, and acceptance, an opening is made for him to move into feeling emotionally safe and secure, which then leads to academic achievement (see Figure 9.1).

Figure 9.1. Relationship drives academic achievement.

If the child is dysregulated and working from a bottom-up control system, one of the most powerful ways to help him shift back to a state of regulation is through the teacher-student connection. Once the child is calm, secure, and back in balance, academic achievement can then take place, as the neocortex is firing and open for learning. In short, *relationship drives academic achievement.*

The traditional model of addressing solely the behavior while ignoring the student's emotional unrest is outdated. The fear of "feeding the monster" that has led teachers to ignore a child due to his negative behavior only gives a child the feeling of being ignored, abandoned, and rejected while imprinting the belief that he does not matter, he is not worthy, and he is not special.

SURVEY SAYS:

"Yes [I liked school], best teacher ever, told me it would be ok, was with me all the time."

By connecting in relationship, the teacher has the capacity to regulate the student in a manner that is far superior to even the best sticker or point charts. When a student is upset and displays a heightened affect, an empathic and regulated teacher's physiology can actually work to shift the student into a regulated state through what is known as entrainment.

Relationship Entrainment. Entrainment is the process of actively changing the natural patterns (vibrations, frequency, or rhythm) of one object to the patterns (vibrations, frequency, or rhythm) of another object. Entrainment was first discovered in 1656 by Christian Huygens. He found that when the pendulums of many grandfather clocks in the same room were started at different rates, they eventually synchronized themselves to the same rhythm. In nature, fireflies grouped together will entrain with one another and blink on and off with the same timing. Female college roommates often have menstrual cycles that synchronize with one another when living in close quarters.

You may have experienced entrainment in your own life when sitting with a friend and having a scintillating conversation. You practically knew what your friend was going to say next or what he was thinking. Time seemed to pass without your awareness. Your brain waves were oscillating synchronously.

The Institute of HeartMath has been a pioneer in this area. For the past thirty years, scientists there have studied the heart's impact on the brain. They have shown that the heart generates forty to sixty times more electrical amplitude than the brain.[2] This electromagnetic field of the heart, also known as the cardiac field, extends about ten feet from outside the body. This cardiac field, touching those within this space, has the power to influence another person's mood, attitude, and feelings. A person's heartbeat can actually be measured in the other person's brainwave, creating a connection between these two people far beyond a surface interaction. Figure 9.2 demonstrates this concept.

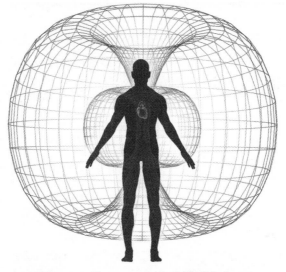

Figure 9.2. Electromagnetic field of the heart.
Reprinted with permission of The Institute of HeartMath.

This dynamic can be exceptionally powerful in the teacher-student relationship. When an emotionally regulated and calm teacher is next to or gently touches the shoulder of a dysregulated and disruptive student, an energy exchange happens. It is through the power of the connection (both physical and psychological) that the teacher becomes entrained with the student and serves as the external regulator for the student. However, for this dynamic between the teacher and student to be effective, it is imperative that the teacher's emotional state be positive. A person's emotional state is what drives the "coherence" of the heart rhythm. Heart coherence is generated from a state of love, gratitude, and happiness. In this state, the waveform is ordered and stable. The result is a patterned and coherent sine wave, as pictured in Figure 9.3.

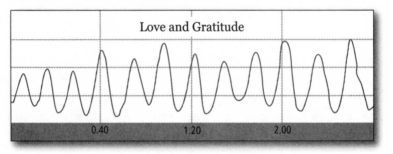

Figure 9.3. Waveform of the heart in a state of love and gratitude.

In the opposite state, when someone is angry and resentful, the waveform is disordered, jagged, and unpredictable, as pictured in Figure 9.4. This type of waveform would only feed negativity and fear into an interaction between a teacher and student, making the situation worse.

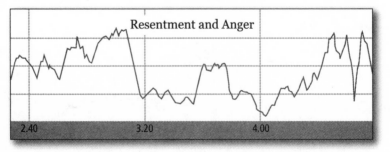

Figure 9.4. Waveform of the heart in a state of resentment and anger.

This is where real power and control reside over a child. A teacher's emotional state truly does have influence over a student and this influence has been underestimated or completely disregarded for far too long. Returning back to a relationship-based model in the classroom is not only a good idea but an idea that has scientific backing and evidence. Hence, teachers must take responsibility for how they are feeling during their time in the classroom. Emotions cannot be suppressed; they have to be processed and acknowledged, otherwise they will show up in resentment and anger, as shown in Figure 9.4.

It is critical for teachers to monitor their thoughts, reactions, and feelings while in the care of their students. No longer can their role be confined to delivering the academic lesson for the day. The evidence on the impact of the heart between two people demands the extension of the teacher as a loving and compassionate human being in the classroom.

The Body Replaces the Sticker Chart. When teachers are in a place of love and gratitude, as pictured in Figure 9.3, they have a powerful tool at their immediate disposal: their body.

Touch. The loving touch of another person can have a profound impact. The sense of touch originates on the skin with the hands being one of the most sensitive areas. The hands are rich in nerve endings and are exceptionally responsive to touch by other human beings.

For younger students, the hand is a safe part of the body to touch and hold. Holding a student's hand has the ability to relax his entire nervous system. For older students, an appropriate touch to the

> **SURVEY SAYS:**
>
> "Being with my teacher makes school better."

shoulder can make a connection with that student that says, "You're okay. I'm here to help you through this." It is a calming and reassuring gesture that speaks at the body level to foster regulation for that student. When the teacher is lecturing and instructing the class, as she walks around the room she can gently and nonchalantly touch Billy's shoulder, while continuing her lecture to the whole class. This instantly creates a connection and regulating gesture to help Billy settle back down, without drawing attention to Billy or interrupting the class.

Breathing. The power of breathing is underestimated, and a teacher's ability to help her students breathe to calm down is underutilized. There are three ways to calm the body's nervous system: (1) input or physical exercise, (2) glucose or food, and (3) oxygen. Of the three, the most effective is oxygen. Breathing has the ability to move someone from an anxious and chaotic state to a calm and regulated state. It can calm the body and the mind.

When a student is getting stressed out and upset, his physical body responds. The heart rate rises, muscles tense, and breathing becomes shallow and rapid. The breath can be used to directly influence these stressful changes, especially when reinforced and demonstrated by a regulated teacher who has a strong relationship with a student. Teachers can incorporate breathing techniques into the regular classroom routine as a preventative measure in controlling behavior, as well as to help calm the student whose nervous system has become charged up.

Nonverbal Communication. It is not always the words that matter when communicating but how the words are delivered. When children are stressed, nonverbal communication, which is processed in the right hemisphere (emotional hemisphere), is received more intensely than verbal communication, which is processed in the left hemisphere. Research shows that the right hemisphere stores the vocabulary for nonverbal affective signals such as facial expressions, emotional tone of voice, and gestures. Thus, it is not what you say that is as important as how you say it.[3]

When the nonverbal communication is incongruent with the verbal message being delivered, it is exceptionally unsetting for Billy and can invoke a fear reaction. For example, if a teacher is trying to be calm and reassuring by saying, "You're okay, Billy," but she has a look of anger and frustration on her face, the outside does not match the inside. This incongruence alerts Billy and in his fear-based mind, he automatically concludes, "This person is unsafe." Thus, the wrong message can unintentionally be conveyed to Billy if the teacher is not mindful of her nonverbal communication. Table 9.1 gives examples of the importance of nonverbal communication with a child like Billy.

Table 9.1. Forms of nonverbal communication

Nonverbal Communication	
Tone of voice	When a teacher raises her voice, Andy knows she is frustrated. Billy believes he is going to get hurt.
Posture	A posture of certainty and confidence conveying, "I can handle you, Billy" creates much more emotional safety for Billy than a defensive and angry posture conveying, "I don't know what to do with you."
Facial expressions	Billy is going to assume even a half-smile means the teacher is mad at him. Andy can interpret subtleties of facial expressions with much more accuracy.
Gestures	If Billy has a history of physical abuse, abrupt hand gestures can be interpreted to mean that he is about to get hit.
Intensity of response	Variations in the pitch and volume of speech will greatly influence whether the message from the teacher will be received as help or as a threat.
Timing and rhythm	When a child is stressed out, he typically needs more time to process language. If the teacher can slow down her speech and deliver her words with a loving rhythm and melody, Billy will have a greater chance of responding positively.
Proximity	Standing too close to Billy, encroaching into his personal space, can sometimes become a threat, even if the intention is to move closer to him in order to soothe him.
Touch	For Andy, soft touch is interpreted as affection, familiarity, sympathy, and other loving feelings. If Billy has had a history of physical or sexual abuse, soft touch in a moment of stress can create reactivity.

Cultural and Personal Beliefs. The qualities that generally define a teacher as a "good teacher" are that she is (1) a good communicator, (2) a good listener, (3) knowledgeable, (4) friendly and respectful, (5) humorous, (6) flexible, (7) patient, and (8) committed to high expectations. These are the overt qualities that can be easily observed in teachers.

Underneath these basic characteristics runs a river of the more covert, nebulous, and obscure characteristics that we as a culture use, as well as what individuals use, to define a good teacher. For example, as the principal is taking another administrator around the school for a tour, he purposefully goes to the classroom where he knows the students will be well behaved. "Here we have Miss Brown's class. She is an excellent teacher. Her students are so attentive." These types of statements form belief systems in us as a society and as individuals that sway us to believe that good behavior from a student directly correlates to a good teacher. Conversely, a poorly behaved or failing student correlates to a bad teacher. In reality, the two are rarely connected and it is a false gauge that can get deeply ingrained into a teacher's subconscious thinking and put undue pressure on her and ultimately the student.

Within this framework, the conversation in a teacher's mind, whether conscious or subconscious, often reflects these thoughts:

- "If Billy performs and achieves, I am a good teacher."
- "I can't coddle him; I'll be a weak teacher."
- "I have to get Billy to behave. I don't want to be seen as a bad teacher."
- "If he doesn't learn to behave now, then he'll flunk out of school by the time he is sixteen. This is my responsibility."
- "I have to make sure he succeeds, otherwise I am a failure."

Throughout the day, the teacher is under pressure at every turn to create the perception that she is a good teacher. When the class is lined up and walking by the principal's office, the teacher is stressing to ensure that Billy does not spontaneously break into a meltdown and create a scene. When her students are going through the cafeteria line, she is stressing to make sure the students are using their manners and being polite. With the pressure of state testing, she is under tremendous strain to have her students perform well so that she will be graded as a good teacher.

This outcome-focused belief system that ties the quality of a teacher to the student's behavior creates undue stress and overwhelm, which then creates problems for both Billy and the teacher. The irony is that the more these two are correlated in a teacher's mind, the more this belief system has the potential for increasing Billy's negative behavior. Billy has a small window of stress tolerance, so the more he feels the pressure to behave and achieve, whether overtly or covertly from his teacher, the more he will crumble in the face of this stress and act out negatively. Figure 9.5 illustrates how this typical scenario develops:

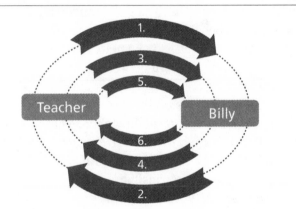

1. Teacher subconsciously correlates Billy's behavior to the effectiveness of being a teacher. She puts stress on Billy to behave.

2. Billy feels this stress and due to his high sensitivity to stress, he acts out.

3. Teacher interprets Billy's misbehavior to mean she is ineffective. This is an uncomfortable feeling for her, so she works harder for Billy to behave in order to settle her own nervous system.

4. Billy feels this stress, cannot sustain his own regulation, and his negative behaviors intensify.

5. The teacher feels worse and moves into feeling overwhelmed, ineffective, unworthy, and increases her intensity toward Billy to get his act together.

6. Billy knows only how to react and is now caught in a negative feedback loop and escalates even more into his negativity.

Figure 9.5. Negative feedback loop between teacher and Billy.

Traditionally, we have asked Billy to be the one to break the negative feedback loop. However, the question begs to be asked, "Between Billy and his teacher, who has the greater amount of flexibility and the greater capacity to make a change?" The answer is the teacher. Billy is constricted, rigid, and familiar with chaos. Change for him means venturing into the unfamiliar, which ignites fear and overwhelm into his system, a system that is already at its breaking point. The solution lies in the teacher both changing her belief system and switching to a framework of self-validation.

First, it is imperative, especially when teaching a child like Billy, for the teacher to never connect her self-worth and effectiveness to a student's behavior. If she is providing the right environment, offering a relationship with the student, and giving understanding to what is driving the student's behavior, she is doing everything necessary. Ultimately, it is the student's responsibility to accept and receive these provisions. She must cut the cord between her effectiveness and the student's behavior.

Second, it is the teacher's personal responsibility to validate herself. It is never Billy's responsibility to make her feel like a good teacher, ever. That is her job. While affirmations from students, colleagues, and administrators are nice, ultimately it is always goes back to being the teacher's responsibility to validate, accept, and love herself. We live in a society and culture where we beg for others to validate us, while in reality the people we are asking to do this for us often do not even do it for themselves.

Billy does not feel like a good student, so it is out of his realm of possibilities to make his teacher feel like a good teacher. He does not validate himself (his belief system says he is unworthy, unlovable, and does not deserve to be on this planet). Therefore, he is in no way capable of validating any adult in his life (parent, teacher, etc.) as effective or capable.

When a teacher knows she is a good teacher and has certainty and confidence in herself, she gives Billy the message that he is unconditionally accepted and that she can handle him. At that moment, there is no more pressure on Billy to be different than anyone but himself. Billy then has more space, with less stress and pressure, to actually be able to make a shift in the right direction. He experiences unconditional love. This is what gives him the ability to feel safe and ultimately be able to shift back into the part of the brain that allows him to make good judgments and choices and thus be the "good" student.

Emotional Awareness. Emotions, both pleasant and unpleasant, are an integral part of every teacher's day. In a recent study identifying teachers' emotional expression with students, it was found that the most frequently experienced pleasant emotion is joy and the most frequently experienced unpleasant emotion is anger. The most influential factor leading to the feeling of joy was student achievement; conversely, the most influential factor leading to the feeling of anger was student disciplinary issues.[4]

With Billy in the classroom, the level of anger experienced by his teacher will typically be much more intense than with Andy. Billy is going to demonstrate negative verbal responses, difficulties following rules, and limitations in his motivation, simply by the nature of who he is. The average frequency of a teacher's experiences of anger will be heightened with these types of dynamics in her classroom.

> **SURVEY SAYS:**
>
> "It would help if the teacher was nicer and wouldn't yell at kids so much."

Students like Billy have a talent for moving a teacher to her deepest, darkest, and most raw emotional states. (Even Mother Teresa would have been challenged to stay calm, loving, and spiritually centered if teaching Billy.) To deal with this intensity, the teacher must operate at a higher level of consciousness and at a greater level of awareness to own and process any anger that surfaces within her. She cannot allow this type of negative emotional flow to be projected back onto Billy or back into the classroom environment—this will only perpetuate the negative behaviors from Billy. The reality is that Billy is challenging. However, this is never a reason for a teacher to unleash her dysregulation back onto a student or into the classroom environment.

"Unfinished Business." The challenge for the teacher is to keep herself regulated and in a state of balance—not an easy task when working with Billy or a room full of Billys. The day in and day out of teaching a student like Billy is difficult on its own. However, teachers also need to be mindful of when their reactions go above and beyond what is appropriate for a particular situation. Teachers have their own personal histories, and it is typically a student like Billy who will be able to trigger a teacher into her own past unresolved issues and experiences.

When a teacher moves from a place of responding to her student to a place of reacting, the issue is no longer about the student. The focus needs to turn back to the teacher. As with any scenario between two people, when one person's reaction is above and beyond the intensity of the moment, something deeper has been triggered.

For instance, if a teacher grew up in a home where she never felt good enough in her parents' eyes, no matter how hard she tried, the same dynamic would surely surface when teaching Billy. Billy has a way, through his negative behaviors, to make her feel as if nothing is working with him, and thus, the teacher would once again be hit with that familiar feeling that she is not good enough.

When unresolved feelings of the past, otherwise known as our "unfinished business," surface later in life, they have the power to put us in a reactive and overly exaggerated anger state. The feelings from the present moment converge with feelings surfacing from the past, and in a matter of milliseconds an internal volcano makes us feel like we are going to explode. The result is the feeling of being emotionally hijacked. The notorious "button" gets pushed. The deepest, most hurtful memories that were once dormant are opened up and an outpouring of anger, even rage, can unfold. Billy, the student who can be as abrasive as sandpaper, quickly becomes the target of this reactivity. Yet when this happens, it has far more to do with the teacher than with Billy, the actual button pusher.

When a teacher feels this reaction starting to boil up within her, the question "What is driving Billy's behavior?" must be turned to the teacher, not in a guilting and blaming way, but in a loving and mindful way. The teacher needs to ask herself:

1. "From where is my reactivity stemming?"
2. "What is keeping me from being in relationship with this student right now?"

Teachers must be aware of how children like Billy have an extraordinary ability to find exactly what triggers them. Instead of being perceived as the difficult student of the classroom, this student needs to be seen as one of the greatest gifts to the classroom. Billy will keep a teacher in her process; he will move her beyond who she is and challenge her to find a deeper sense of self and a deeper sense of her love for teaching. Granted, the delivery of this gift from Billy could use some tweaking. The difficulty of his behaviors should never be minimized. The bottom line, though, is that when the teacher can view Billy as normal for his life experiences and when she can embrace her own opportunity for internal growth and healing, Billy begins each day with a new message that he is worthy and acceptable, and thus, a chance at academic success opens for Billy.

Window of Stress Tolerance. Just as the window of stress tolerance (discussed in chapter 2) applies to Billy, the same holds true for teachers. At the beginning of the school year, after the teacher has had a rejuvenating summer vacation, her window is at its maximum (see left side of Figure 9.6).

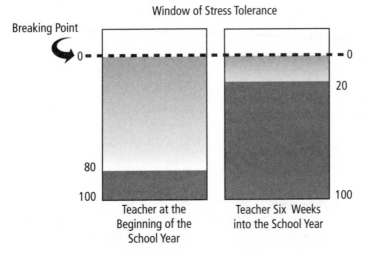

Figure 9.6. Teacher's window of stress tolerance.

Six weeks later, after working through challenging behaviors with Billy, day in and day out, even the most patient of teachers has the ability to be worn down (see right side of Figure 9.6). Teacher self-care is vital to staying open to being in relationship with students. When any of us are stressed, dysregulated, and frustrated, we close down to relationship. The space is gone. Therefore, maintaining a relationship-focused classroom mandates that teachers take good care of themselves. They must work to keep their window large. When the window becomes small, as in the right side of Figure 9.6, trying to stay in a place of understanding, acceptance, and tolerance for Billy will prove futile.

It is not about the teacher having more self-discipline, tenacity, or fortitude. When a teacher is worn down, she is worn down. There is nothing else to give. Billy will feel this decrease in the teacher's window and it will increase his arousal system. He will react to this and become fearful and feel as if another relationship in his life has failed him, triggering him into feeling abandoned, rejected, and forgotten. This will then manifest into a rise in negative behaviors, and once again Billy will go spiraling downward into an abyss of fear, overwhelm, and pain.

Solutions for Staying Regulated. Teachers have a tendency to be natural caregivers. While this is a wonderful trait, most of the time they forget to take care of themselves. And sometimes the bigger issue is that they have never given themselves permission to take care of themselves. If you are a teacher, you need to take care of yourself first, then your students. It is not about being selfish; it is about being selfless in the giving of yourself. You cannot give something you have not received. Take care of yourself in order to take care of your students.

If you are a teacher, here are some guidelines for making sure you are regulated and able to stay in a loving space for your students:

> ### SURVEY SAYS:
>
> "Kind teachers who have a nice voice, even when you make them upset they stay calm and have a calm voice."

Ask the Right Question. One of the best ways to stay regulated with a large window is to stay in a place of understanding by viewing Billy's behavior from Billy's perspective. Asking the right question, "What is driving Billy's behavior?" keeps you in a loving perspective.

When Billy's behaviors "make sense," the frustration level remains low and there is room for relationship.

Seek Support. You need support and you should not do this alone. Sometimes it takes asking, so break the barrier and ask and create support around you. Support in the classroom from paraprofessionals and volunteer parents can make all the difference. Teachers need the support of administrators who understand what trauma does to a child's physiology and brain. Working together instead of questioning or judging teachers is everything.

Validate Yourself. Continually disconnect your students' level of achievement and behavior from the effectiveness of you as a teacher. "It's Not About Me" should be in your mind's eye all of the time when working with Billy. It is about Billy's history, not about you, the teacher. If you do not validate yourself as a good teacher, others will not believe you are a good teacher, either. When you have confidence in yourself, others will see you differently and see your strengths also. Remember, Muhammad Ali told everyone he was the greatest and he became the greatest. Believe in yourself, live in your heart, and know that your best is good enough.

Take Care of Yourself at School. During the school day, take time to breathe and slow down. Slow down. S-l-o-w—d-o-w-n. This is exceptionally difficult when you feel pressured to get through a lesson plan, but the reality is that the more you slow down, the easier it is for your students to process the information and not get overwhelmed. Doing so will also help you to keep your nervous system in check. If you have support in the classroom and someone can cover for you, let your students know you need a "time-out" to settle yourself back down. It is a wonderful way to model personal responsibility to your students. Eat a healthy lunch and do not skip lunch; feed your physical body to keep yourself physically regulated. When your students are in a special class like physical education or music, take five or ten minutes to meditate or get some fresh air instead of devoting the entire time to lesson plans and grading papers. When you have free time, listen to music that calms you. Drink water throughout the day. Staying hydrated is one of the best ways to keep your energy level at its peak.

Apply Self-Care Outside of School. Take care of your body, your oldest friend, and be kind to it. Exercise decreases your internal stress level while simultaneously increasing your energy level. Include activities in your life that are fun, give you enjoyment, and are meaningful. Also, keep yourself socially connected with friends who are not part of the school environment. If you are working with trauma all day, you have to keep yourself connected to the "real" world where people think clearly and are emotionally stable.

Understand Trauma. The field of neuroscience is growing every day and the information available is expanding immensely. Keep yourself informed and current on the new understanding as to how trauma impacts a child's nervous system and how it will manifest in your classroom. One of the most powerful ways to keep yourself regulated and patient is through one word: understanding. Albert Einstein said it best, "Peace cannot be kept by force; it can only be achieved by understanding." Understanding is a teacher's pivotal force in sustainability.

Love Yourself. You are a gift to your students. Your ability to love and validate yourself, without asking the same from your students in return, is vital. The Billys in your classroom do not have the ability to reciprocate this to you. Sometimes it takes digging deeper within yourself, on those especially difficult days, to tap into the well within you to hear that inner affirming voice, letting you know you are a good teacher and that you are doing amazing work. Rest on your purpose in life, without expecting Billy's behavior to provide the gold star that you deserve. Love yourself enough to give that to yourself and let Billy simply be Billy. Remember, it is not about you!

CHAPTER TEN

Homework

■

*I like a teacher who gives you something to take
home to think about besides homework.*
~ Lily Tomlin

"**I**f they don't learn to do their homework now, they'll never make it in college." These were the exact words of a teacher speaking to a parent about the necessity of homework. She was adamant the children in her classroom learn to be responsible and self-disciplined. While it might be possible to fathom this statement coming from a high school teacher or perhaps a middle school teacher, it is hard to believe it came from a kindergarten teacher. That would equate to the absolute need for a five-year-old to go home after a full six hours of school and then do more work.

Homework has become the norm for children in kindergarten through high school. Homework is viewed as an intellectual discipline to establish good study habits and develop good character. Teachers use it to ease time constraints on the amount of material that can be covered in class and to supplement and reinforce the lessons covered in school. Homework is intended to foster student initiative, independence, and responsibility.

> ### SURVEY SAYS:
> ───────────
> Do you think homework helps
> you learn more?
>
> "No it takes time away from
> my family."

While the thoughts and ideas behind homework are well intended, logical, and reasonable, how do they actually play out in the reality of most school-age children? If you took a video camera into 100,000 homes after school and filmed what was happening during homework time, what would you see? Intellectual discipline or rebellious chaos? As many parents would testify, you would see the latter—rebellious chaos. In fact, for Billy, you would see rebellious chaos unmatched by any other activity children are asked to perform. You would see Billy yelling and tearing up his homework. You would see pencils flying, books being slammed, and tearful cries and threats of *"I hate you— I'm not doing this homework and you can't make me!"* Billy would rather go to the dentist than do his homework. In addition to seeing Billy exhibiting negative behaviors, you would also see parents hitting their window of stress tolerance. You would see parents reverting to being two-year-olds as they reach new levels of exasperation. And all of this would be in the name of "learning."

Articles and books with new coined phrases such as "homework stress" and "homework wars" are available for parents seeking answers to this dilemma. Most of the expert advice centers on how to get children to do their work, but focuses on the outcome of children walking into class with their homework in hand to turn in to their teacher.

The combination of the words "homework"/"stress" and "homework"/"war" warrants a moment to consider and explore. The juxtaposition of these words can in no way foster our children's love for learning. First, we know from scientific research that stress causes short-term memory loss. An oversecretion of stress hormones adversely affects the brain and can prevent the brain from laying down a new memory or accessing already existing memories.[1] No one can learn when stressed out. Second, war is about winning, which implies someone will lose. When homework becomes a battle, everybody loses; there are no winners. Learning is supposed to be fun, not a conflict or fight for survival.

SURVEY SAYS:

Do you think homework helps you learn more?

"No. Homework causes stress and stress causes nightmares."

Traditional View

Traditionally, homework polices in schools throughout the United States have been written with a high level of rigidity and fraught with fear. Strict policies and procedures are described in detail to ensure the completion of out-of-school assignments for the students. Here is such an example:

> *"Homework is assigned every evening in every subject. This includes weekends, holidays, and vacation days. If a parent is told or believes that their son or daughter does not have nightly homework, instead of accepting an explanation from the student, please call the school immediately! The preparation of homework is a shared responsibility—the student-parent-teacher. Please call the principal as soon as possible if you sense any kind of problem concerning the homework. Also, where homework is not completed or is inadequately prepared, parents will be called by the teacher. Continued failure to prepare and turn in homework will be considered a deficiency that will affect the student's final grade."*

Typically, the language chosen to lay out homework policies is militant and creates a feeling of "us" (the school) against "you" (the student). As the example above shows, it is reactive in nature and exudes a power-and-control tone. A "do not even try to get away without doing your homework because we will catch you" fear-based message is given to students.

Traditional parental guidelines for helping children with homework usually focus on logistical procedures to follow at home. Recommendations include monitoring television viewing, establishing a specific homework time, planning a homework schedule with the child, and allowing free time only when assignments are completed.

Educators place a tremendous amount of emphasis around the lesson of responsibility and homework. The two are tied closely together, as if they are one and the same: "Children need to know early on that homework is a responsibility; everything else is a privilege." Homework in this traditional perspective takes precedence over extracurricular activities such as music lessons, martial arts, or social activities. One educator from Brown University, who represents the mindset of so many of our children's educators, says that getting homework done is the single most important job a child has. She states, "Parents who put extracurricular activities ahead [of homework] have it backwards."[2]

Parenting experts, especially those specializing in working with oppositional children with trauma histories, stress the importance of making certain that homework be 100% the child's responsibility beginning as early as first grade. In the traditional view, it is thought that children like Billy purposely seek battles and are relentless about control. Thus, when the parent engages in a battle over homework, the child will automatically fight it and nothing will be accomplished. Instead, these experts recommend that the parent not interact in the homework process. They believe that when the child learns that the natural consequence of not doing homework is an automatic zero or F, the child will move toward improvement by putting out effort. This process of the child putting out effort is seen as a way to build a child's self-esteem. Additionally, children "must believe the truth, that an education is vital to their success in their adult life, and that their brain must have exercise to develop properly."[3]

Professionals helping families struggling through homework issues traditionally suggest writing a contract between the parent and the child. The contract includes both the parent's and the child's participation and approval. A copy is kept in the child's file at school and a copy is given to the family to post at home.[4]

Books written on helping children with their homework suggest the parent help only when the parent is not angry or frustrated with the child. They also suggest the parent help only when the child can describe the teacher's instructions—this is to ensure that the child understands the importance of paying attention to teachers. Other books recommend that the parent hold rigid boundaries of "work before play," with no exceptions, and that the rules be enforced matter-of-factly.[5]

Some experts working from the traditional perspective recommend that to prevent a child from becoming dependent on the parent, the parent should avoid the habit of sitting at the table as the child does his homework. ("If your child needs you to sit with him, something is wrong.")[6] This view also stresses that the parent should not do the homework for the child, because when this happens the child misses the point of homework, that "homework is meant to be practice. That means you are allowed to make mistakes."[7]

New View

The Brain. As previously discussed, the neocortex gives us higher cognitive abilities such as alertness, attention, planning, memory, and the ability to regulate appropriate social behaviors (i.e., emotional and impulse control). In children, this part of the brain is still developing and will not finish developing until they are at least twenty-five years old. Research over the past ten years clearly shows that stress impairs this part of the brain in adults and children.[8] Plainly stated, this means when children become stressed out, they cannot think clearly. Asking children to do homework during this time is a setup for failure and frustration.

The traditional suggestions around homework do not account for this finding. The solutions given are cognitively based. They assume the child is in a position to think clearly through his choices. Yet if Billy cannot think clearly, policies and procedures will make no sense and certainly have no impact on motivating him. In fact, policies and procedures typically create more stress and negatively impact Billy's sense of motivation.

> **SURVEY SAYS:**
>
> Do you think homework helps you learn more?
>
> "No, because it just fries your brain and doesn't allow time for breaks and bond[ing] with your family."

Cause-and-effect thinking requires upper-level brain capacity. Traditional homework techniques assume a child who fails because he has not done his homework will correlate the two together and come to a logical conclusion. It assumes a child will understand that to pass, he must study and do homework, and thus motivation will be established. It also assumes the child wants to pass. Billy already believes he is a failure and unworthy, so failing grades will merely confirm these beliefs. Failure will only widen and deepen his internal pit of overwhelm, keeping him trapped and feeling more worthless.

Traditional thinking around homework also fails to consider Billy's emotional state. It views children as logical machines or computers and suggests parents respond in this mechanical way as well. Children, especially Billy, do not operate by "if-then" statements. An if-then statement is just what the name implies. It is a statement that proves if something happens, then something else will follow: "If I don't do my homework, then I will fail." This may be logical thinking to an adult, yet from Billy's perspective and from his level of brain development, it does not compute. Homework needs to support Billy's brain development, not punish it for being underdeveloped.

How can we continue to punish and blame Billy for not being able to think clearly through homework issues when we know from scientific evidence this is a perfectly normal response? Putting stress on Billy to do homework after a long day of being stressed out at school is like trying to pump water from a dry well. There is nothing more to give.

SURVEY SAYS:

Do you think homework helps you learn more?

"No because homework should be school work because at home you're supposed to spend time with your family."

The Homework. In addition to the research on the brain, research on the issue of homework itself is quite revealing. In fact, it is stunning. Research from the Institute of Education in the UK found that homework causes such friction between parents and children—especially middle-class families, where concerns about a child's future can lead to a climate of pressure to succeed—that any potential educational benefits are lost.[9] Alfie Kohn, author of *The Homework Myth*, states:

"There is absolutely no evidence of any academic benefit from assigning homework in elementary or middle school. For younger students, in fact, there isn't even a correlation between whether children do homework (or how much they do) and any meaningful measure of achievement. At the high school level, the correlation is weak and tends to disappear when more sophisticated measures are applied. Meanwhile, no study has ever substantiated the belief that homework builds character or teaches good study habits."[10]

Research has also shown that the most effective homework is "prep," where children are asked to prepare something for an upcoming lesson.

Emotional Regulation. When children become upset and demonstrate frustration, anger, and even hostility toward the parent or their homework, they have exhausted their window. Forcing Billy through his window will result in him losing his love for learning. It will also result in losing the opportunity to build a strong, loving, and safe parent-child relationship. Nothing is ever worth losing this relationship—nothing.

John Bowlby, in his work in the area of attachment theory, described how the mother is the regulator for her child.[11] As discussed in chapter 2, by sitting with your child in a state of calm acceptance for the struggle he is having, you are resonating positive energy through your physiology; you are being the "thermostat" to help your child shift back into a state of balance.

Instead of creating more dysregulation for Billy and being a counterforce in the connection with him, think about becoming a positive and loving influence to the level of regulation within Billy. You have the power to counterbalance the dysregulation by your state of regulation. In the late 1800s, Walt Whitman wrote about this in his poem, "Song of the Open Road." In lines 139 and 140, he writes:

I and mine do not convince by arguments, similes, rhymes; we convince by our presence.

What is exciting is that now we have the scientific evidence to back such a poetic truth.

The traditional perspective regarding homework—"If your child needs you to sit with him, something is wrong"—fails to take into consideration the scientific proof that children with high sensitivities to stress have difficulty self-regulating. Of course they need you to sit with them. One of the best solutions for Billy, who is chronically dysregulated, is to have the parent sit with him (as long as the parent can stay in a balanced state of regulation) during homework time. It also requires that the parent understand and acknowledge the level of fear that homework presents to Billy.

For children with histories of abandonment, neglect, and rejection, facing a worksheet of homework can be like sitting down to hear a jury's verdict. It is as if that piece of paper is going to determine whether the child lives or dies. Children at this level of survival fight against doing such an assignment for hours on end. Homework time is a life-threatening event. The parent's perspective—"It is only a simple sheet of math problems"—fails to understand the threat such a math sheet presents to the child. It takes the parent understanding and seeing what a significant threat homework can be for a child.

For Billy, mistakes mean, "I'm bad. And if I'm bad, you won't love me. And if you don't love me, I will die." It literally comes down to such a survival-based interpretation when considering homework. If picking up a pencil meant that your life might be over at any second, you too would fight against doing such an assignment.

Children like Billy who live at this level are unconcerned about their future. In their eyes, their future does not even exist. Believing that they have the capacity to "believe the truth, that an education is vital to their success in their adult life, and that their brain must have exercise to develop properly" is unreasonable and far beyond their capacity.[12]

Remember, Billy lives only for the moment. His world is black and white—here and now. All his resources are focused on the moment at hand to survive and ensure his safety. Long-term planning is part of the brain's higher-order thinking, which is outside the realm of Billy's primal brain activity. Expecting Billy to develop and engage in this type of thinking comes from an adult perspective, void of any understanding of Billy's level of survival thinking.

Solutions. The best homework solution would be to place a cease-and-desist order on homework altogether, though this may not be possible. Solutions that are possible—those that decrease stress around homework and simultaneously help Billy regulate during these stressful times—are the focus of the rest of this chapter.

Have Billy Teach You. Those who teach are the greatest students. When you take interest in Billy's schoolwork, you are giving him the message that what he is learning is important. This is also an opportunity to join Billy in his world, an opportunity lost far too often. When parents jump into a child's world, the child feels important, special, and loved, which then correlates to building both a strong foundation and secure attachment with the child.

Help Billy Regulate. Teach Billy how to take deep breaths to calm his neurological system. Interrupt negative feedback loops by taking breaks with him. Go for a walk, play with the family dog, blow bubbles (for breathing), or have a snack together. Keep in mind that none of his resistance is intentional. It is not against you. It is an internal battle going on within his heart; it is a manifestation of his own self-rejection. Sometimes this self-rejection rears its ugly head against the parent because it feels better for Billy to project it onto you rather than feel it himself.

Break the Assignment Down. Understand that Billy is feeling so overwhelmed that he cannot do the work. It is not that he won't; he simply can't. Relate this to your own experiences of being overwhelmed in your work. You walk into the office and see 150 emails to answer, numerous phone calls to return, an overflowing inbox, and a note from your boss reminding you that an extensive report is due at noon. How do you feel? What do you do to overcome this feeling? Maybe you get up and go to the break room and get some coffee (a regulatory beverage).

So for Billy, break up the twenty spelling words and start with just five. Yes, five. Five is better than none. Five is better than pencils being broken or paper being shredded. Work to build up Billy's

SURVEY SAYS:

Do you think homework helps you learn more?

"Yes, cause sometimes you get homework that you don't know and then your parents help you with it."

window of homework tolerance. Eventually he will be able to do ten, then fifteen, and then twenty. Trust in the process and stop pushing Billy beyond his capabilities.

We all learned to walk before we could run. For children to find their way through homework assignments, we must realize it is a sequential process. Baby steps now will lead to giant leaps in the future.

Give Emotional Space. Many children have not learned to use their voice or they have not been given permission to use their voice. Instead, they fight and rebel against homework assignments.

We as parents, fearful our child will not pass or, worse, that we will look like bad parents because our child is not completing his homework, fight back with controlling measures to save face with the teacher. It takes the parents shifting out of their own fear and stepping into Billy's fear. The fight Billy is putting on is saying, "I can't do this anymore. Stop controlling me and stop making me do this because it is only making me worse!" Think about how it would feel if your boss pushed you and pushed you and fought you over getting an assignment completed. How would it feel to be controlled like this? You would probably fight back—or simply quit. It is no different for Billy.

Trying to convince Billy he needs to do his homework will only breed more resistance. Giving him logical reasons why he needs to care about his homework and his education will leave him feeling isolated and on his own to defend his position. Billy needs you to listen to him before he can listen to you. Here is an example of an interaction that helped a real-life Billy get through his resistance to homework:

> **SURVEY SAYS:**
>
> Do you think homework helps you learn more?
>
> "No—I learned all day, when I get home I want to play."

Mom: Let's look at today's schedule and you tell me what time you would like to do your homework."

Billy: "I don't care about any schedule because I'm not doing my homework."

Mom: "Wow. You sound like you're quite upset, Billy."

Billy: "Of course I'm upset. I hate doing homework."

Mom: "I can see that."

Billy: "Why do I have to spend my playtime doing homework? I'm at school all day long."

Mom: "That is hard, isn't it?"

Billy: "I hate it. And you can't make me do it. I don't care if I fail."

Mom: "That's how hard it is for you, isn't it?"

Billy: "I'm sick of it all."

Mom: "It's hard doing all of this on your own, isn't it Billy?"

Billy: (Nodding his head to say, "Yes, it is!)

Mom: "What can I do to help you, sweetheart?"

Billy: "I don't know."

Mom: "Maybe I can sit down with you and help you, just today?"

Billy: "Maybe."

Mom: "This is too much to have to handle on your own. I'm here to help you through it."

Billy: "Okay."

Billy needs support and validation from his parents. He does have the ability to make good choices. He needs to know he is understood and supported, not judged and controlled. It takes the power of the parent-child relationship to help steer Billy in the right direction.

Reduce Stress. Eliminate stressors in the home environment that might be stress inducing and creating more overwhelm for Billy. Additionally, see if there are any factors at school creating more stress around homework for Billy. Many times just the thought of a consequence for not finishing homework, such as not being able to go to recess or being singled out from the other students, is enough to create such a black cloud around Billy that his level of stress becomes completely overwhelming and it stifles any ability he may have to complete the work. Ironically, consequences intended to motivate become the block that decreases or entirely stifles motivation.

Speak with Billy's teacher and explain that Billy has a high sensitivity to stress and that the fear-driven consequence is creating a negative situation for him. Some teachers resist adjusting their

SURVEY SAYS:

Do you think homework helps
you learn more?

"Yes, because your family helps
you with what you don't know and
I get to do it with my family."

policies for one student, saying, "If I make an exception for Billy, I'll have to make an exception for every child." The reality is that not every child is having this difficulty, so not every child needs this exception. Meeting the needs of one child to ensure a successful educational experience should always be the priority.

Find Different Times for Homework. Allow time after coming home from school for Billy to reconnect with the parent instead of insisting he complete his homework right away. Yes, it would make life easier to have the homework done and not have to worry about it for the rest of the evening. However, the reality is that Billy may not be able to do this.

Relate this to your own experiences. When you get off work, do you feel like pulling out your briefcase and sitting down to do more work? Or if you are a stay-at-home parent, when you finish cooking the last meal of the day, do you feel like spending the next hour or two in the kitchen drumming up a new recipe? No. You are depleted of your internal sense of motivation and drained of creativity. You need to be refueled. The same is true for Billy.

Have Billy set what time of the evening he would like to come back to finish the homework. If Billy continues to struggle in the evenings with completing the homework, ask the teacher for the flexibility for Billy to complete the homework on the weekends. Weekends are less stressful, and the relaxed atmosphere can create a drastically different environment for Billy to find his way through the stress of homework.

Reduce the Pressure. Billy's educational expectations need to be equivalent to that which matches his abilities. If your family of origin stressed academics as paramount to success, examine these beliefs objectively to determine if you are putting this past family stress on Billy.

Accept that Billy is doing the best he can do for this moment. Trust that he has the capacity to do more and know without a doubt that that time will come. It takes meeting Billy where he is to help him develop a stronger self-regulatory system and find his own internal sense of motivation. Forcing and threatening will only block progress and create resentment toward you and his entire educational career.

Work Through Problems with Billy. Children can learn by demonstration as well as by doing the work themselves. If Billy is resisting doing the work by himself, do it with him. In fact, if his fear drives so much resistance to the homework process, complete the homework for him. Yes. You read that correctly. Do it for him. Simply ask Billy to sit with you and talk through the problem as you complete it.

This may challenge your values and belief system to the core and that is good because this means you are opening up to the truth about homework. Homework is intended to help children, not hurt them. By going as far as doing the work for Billy, trust that he is still learning. He is learning the academic material by your teaching. Your fear might be saying, "No, what Billy will learn is how to manipulate me into doing his homework for him." This is the fear that keeps us from making homework time different.

By doing the homework for him, you are creating a positive homework experience for Billy, free of stress and threat. Billy will learn the important fact

> ### SURVEY SAYS:
>
> ---
>
> Do you think homework helps you learn more?
>
> "Yes, because you get help from your parents and it is quieter at home."

that you are committed to helping him and you will take every step possible to ensure his success. This is the ultimate lesson in learning responsibility—having someone take responsibility for you teaches you how to take responsibility for yourself in the future.

Within a short time, you will find that Billy actually wants to do the homework himself instead of you doing it. Children do not like sitting and watching. They are doers. They like to participate; they do not like to be bystanders. How many children do you see sitting on a park bench just watching the other children play? None. They want to play too. Give Billy the jump-start to doing his homework and help him break the barrier he has been fighting to maintain for protection. Make it safe. Make it fun. Create joy in stressful situations.

SURVEY SAYS:

Do you think homework helps
you learn more?

"No. I need some playtime so
I can focus better in school."

The bottom line is that low-stress environments keep the brain calm and regulated. The people around Billy, the intensity of the requirements and expectations, and the level of emotional openness will influence the effectiveness of the environment for Billy. In the past, too much emphasis has been placed on getting children to complete the work without considering any of these factors. Here is a true story of a mom who implemented the ideas in this chapter around homework, and six years later her "Billy" is excelling and the daily homework battles are nonexistent:

> When my Billy was in the fourth grade, just about every homework page had tear tracks and an overabundance of anger and frustration. I decided that I was no longer going to sacrifice my child's childhood for a school policy so I made it a family rule to put relationship first and schoolwork second. It was then that I began doing the homework with Billy. Sometimes just the first few lines or problems of the homework were my handwriting; other times the entire sheet was in my handwriting. On good days, Billy would take over and do it all himself. On the days that we struggled, I would attach a Post-It Note saying, "As you can tell, this was rough. I ended up being the scribe, but I assure you he sat next to me and the work and answers are his." Billy is now in tenth grade and is enrolled in all honors classes and does his homework on his own. But more important than this, he is an honorable and loving person who lives from a place of love, not fear.

Creating negative experiences around education and learning for our children is a tragedy. No homework assignment is ever worth sacrificing a child's self-worth or suffocating a child's natural desire to explore and learn. When approaching the task of homework, stay focused on helping your child move forward not backward in his educational career. Stay attuned to both your regulation and Billy's level of regulation. And most of all, when fear overcomes love in the connection between you and your child, homework time is officially over for the day.

CHAPTER ELEVEN

Social and Emotional Issues

■

What we learn to do, we learn by doing.
~ Thomas Jefferson

S ocial relationships are central to the happiness, self-esteem, and sense of belonging for children. When a child masters social skills, he is able to initiate, build, and maintain positive peer relationships. Additionally, mastery of social skills directly influences a child's academic performance. Deficits in social interaction skills interfere with learning, teaching, and a child's sense of self. The bottom line is that a child's social competence correlates to his peer acceptance, teacher acceptance, academic success, and overall emotional well-being.

If a child is not doing well socially (or academically), a strong emotional component is also at play. Every day children return home from school in tears because they were rejected or made fun of by another child. On the extreme, one of the prime causes of teen suicide is social pressure. Hence, the discussion of a child's social development must also include the child's emotional development as well. The two are married; one cannot exist without the other.

Traditional View

For children like Billy, social equals emotional. Billy's response system is so overly stressed, it does not allow him to think clearly during difficult social moments. He reacts without thinking, his behaviors fall outside of what is socially acceptable, he gets into trouble for acting inappropriately, he feels bad and stupid (reinforcing an already established negative belief system), and he is unable to learn due to the heightened level of stress in his system. Negative downward spirals such as this have not been adequately addressed through the traditional mindset of our educational system.

The traditional view asks, "How do we get Billy to change his social behavior?" This question fails miserably for Billy. Traditionally, social skills have been taught at the intellectual and cognitive levels, not taking into account the full extent to which social interactions evoke emotional responses. The traditional approach has been designed for the child like Andy—the child who has the ability to think clearly and remain regulated when challenged emotionally.

One classic technique taught to children is "Stop and Think." There are two problems with this for Billy. First, he has no brakes and cannot stop. Second, Billy cannot think. He feels. And what he feels comes from a deep place of survival. The result is that he reacts automatically before his brain even has a chance to think.

In Table 11.1, the left-hand column lists other traditional techniques that children are taught in order to improve their social skills. For the Billys of the classroom, these techniques will fail them almost every time. The right-hand column gives insight into why they are inadequate.

Socials skills techniques are typically taught through worksheets and cognitive processing. Billy will be able to comprehend these ideas and answer the questions appropriately when he is in a calm and regulated place. However, in the midst of the moment, when he is upset with his friend Andy, Billy will become emotionally charged. He is no longer operating from a top-down control system. Billy's thinking is no longer rational, logical, or objective. He is working from his midbrain—from a bottom-up control. Everything from the cognitive discussion he may have had earlier about how to respond appropriately is inaccessible. Instead, he reacts from a self-protective manner, with no consideration for the future or for others' feelings.

Billy's internal responses, as shown in Table 11.1, are far from cognitive. They stem from a blueprint of fear. The traditional approach has been unsuccessful for Billy because it does not get to the core of what is driving his lack of social skills. It aims to retrain Billy from a cognitive level while all along, ignoring and not even acknowledging the vast emotional undercurrent of abandonment and rejection.

Table 11.1. The ineffectiveness of traditional social skills techniques for Billy

Social Skills Techniques Taught to Students	Billy's Mindset
1. Walk away.	I'm in survival and I have gone into a "fight" response. Walking away is not even an option in my mind.
2. Talk to the other person in a calm way.	I have no ability to self-regulate. I'll yell and make my point known to you. I will NEVER again have someone treat me like garbage.
3. Talk to someone about how you feel.	Every time in the past when I've expressed myself, I have been minimized or told how I should feel differently.
4. Ask someone for help in solving the problem.	Nobody is safe in my eyes, not even the teachers. I trust NOBODY. I'm on my own and I'll take care of this on my own.
5. Find your "Happy Place" inside you and calm down.	There is no "Happy Place" inside of me. There is only an internal volcano going on within me. I'm doing an amazing job containing it all ... what I need is reassurance and emotional safety.
6. An apology is a good way to have the last word.	Nobody ever apologized to me for anything. I was always the one who got blamed. Making an apology would make me feel like it is my fault, once again.
7. It is never as bad it seems. Keep things in proportion and don't create a mountain out of a molehill. Toughen up and stop being so sensitive.	It is a BIG deal to me and it needs to be a big deal to you. I'm not going to sit back and take it anymore. I'm going to make sure you know it is a big deal, no matter the consequences.

New View

The new question for addressing Billy's social skills needs to be, "What is driving Billy's inability to socialize appropriately?" By asking this question, the root cause can be addressed instead of simply piling cognitive thoughts on top of an incredibly powerful undercurrent of fear, rejection, and abandonment.

Three Answers. There are essentially three answers to this question: (1) Billy is socially immature, (2) Billy is not a "social thinker," and (3) Billy is not only scared of rejection, he is terrified of rejection.

Social Immaturity. Billy's chronological age does not match his social or emotional age. Because of the interruption in his developmental path, he is arrested both socially and emotionally. If Billy is eight years old chronologically but five years old socially and emotionally, this can be likened to putting a kindergartener in the playground with third graders. Billy would be "eaten alive." Billy would become threatened and go into fight-or-flight response. In fight mode, he would act aggressively and fight with the other children. Any sense of "that is not nice" would be gone from his perspective because "being nice" would not matter. That is the nature of survival. The only person who matters at that moment of survival is Billy—nobody else. If Billy goes into flight mode, he would distance himself from the other children. He would be in one corner of the playground, oblivious to the other children and make no initiation to interact. This is Billy's hypo-aroused way of socially protecting himself from the overwhelm he experiences surrounded by other children. He is not being anti-social; rather, he is protecting himself and creating distance to decrease his overwhelm.

"Social Thinker." Children like Billy missed the critical early years of being lovingly held and nurtured by a primary caregiver. While these experiences are designed to meet a child's physical needs, so much more than the obvious is being met. Andy had the experience of someone connecting with him at a deeply profound social and emotional level. The caregiver was able to relate to Andy, read his social communication cues, and create emotional safety in the context of relationship with

him. In response, Andy learned to read his caregiver's social cues. His journey of developing social and emotional intelligence began on track.

Billy, on the other hand, missed all the above in his early years. Now as a student in the classroom, he is socially and emotionally deficient. The part of his brain that is designed to interpret social cues is consequently wired differently. His teachers and peers become easily impatient with him for making inappropriate social comments, not making eye contact, and simply being "a little off."

SURVEY SAYS:

"I wish that other kids understood my disability better, so I would have more friends."

Just as a child with dyslexia cannot make sense of the letters he reads on a page, a child with social deficiencies cannot make sense of social cues being given by peers and teachers. Pioneering research on nonverbal communication conducted by Albert Mehrabian, Ph.D., established that 55% of communication is received through facial and body expression, 38% is through the tone of voice and volume, and only 7% is through the feelings and attitudes in the words spoken.[1] It is not so much the words used but the way in which they are used that we understand another person's communication.

Billy may hear the words but does not easily make sense of them. His responses can therefore be inappropriate. Teachers often see children like Billy as deliberately obstinate or rude in class. This misinterpretation leads to Billy being punished for something that was not intentional but simply a deficiency in his development.

Fear of Rejection. The fear of being rejected is a theme that runs through all of us, no matter our backgrounds or walks of life. Test this out by picking up the phone and doing some cold calling. The fear reaction you have when you first pick up the phone and dial a stranger will not only be a thought in your mind but a physical reaction at the body level.

Children with histories of rejection through past trauma experiences live in this state of fear every moment of every day at school. While their fear may be merely a perception in the mind, it is absolutely real to them and will interfere with their ability to focus, excel in the classroom, and socially engage with other students. For example, Billy may have a teacher who is genuinely kind and loving, yet in his black-

and-white thinking, all adults are a threat. He believes a different reality than what he is living.

Billy is not only fearful of being rejected by his peers (and his teachers), he is terrified of it. This, combined with his lack of emotional maturity and deficits in social thinking, makes for a child who can appear rude, disobedient, or withdrawn. Ironically, the fear of being rejected is playing out to ensure that Billy is being rejected.

Many times, however, the fear of rejection will play out in the complete opposite way. Billy has learned from a fear-based place how to manipulate people and engage with people in a smooth, attuned, and almost adult-like fashion. Billy's fear of being rejected or ostracized has actually created a child with an overdeveloped ability to "fit in." He is able to sum people up quickly and socially maneuver himself throughout the day to ensure he is liked and accepted. This is the Billy who comes home with the "Citizenship Award." The teachers rave about how he is a model child, and they tell the parents how they wish all their students were like Billy. Yet when Billy arrives home, he completely unravels and becomes grossly reactive and rejecting to his parents. He held himself together for the entire school day playing the "game" of socialization (in order to survive) and is exhausted. By the time he comes home, he has reached his window of tolerance, explodes, and releases the social tension that has been building all day. His parents become the receivers of this unloading, almost a Dr. Jekyll and Mr. Hyde situation, that feels unsettling and quite rejecting for them.

Some children release this stress onto the parents because they have established a stronger sense of emotional safety with their parents compared to people at school. These children inherently know their parents will accept them, no matter their behavior. Thus, the parents find themselves on the receiving end of this stress. The dichotomy of the two extremes can make it as if the parent and teacher are describing a completely different child.

Other children are threatened by the parent-child relationship. As much as they desire the connection with the parent, this relationship is also an enormous threat. No one can hurt a child, whether emotionally, mentally, or physically, more than the parent. It is by nature that this relationship is to offer the child more love, acceptance, and validation than any other relationship, but in the course of reality, the opposite becomes very true.

When Billy becomes "split" among two developing personalities between school and home, it is exceptionally unhealthy to his development of the self. This splitting is a dissociative behavior; it is a creative and helpful way (from the child's perspective) for him to deal with the overwhelm, challenges, and fear he experiences. However, it is a maladaptive response that he is developing with great skill that needs to be interrupted and addressed. The teachers and parents need to work together as a team to provide a consistent environment between home and school along with open and direct communication. If the teachers and parents remain disconnected, Billy will have a greater chance of doing the same.

The Four L's. Many students simply need to "start over" and begin with the basics of social behaviors. They have not learned to interact in ways that elicit positive responses, nor have they learned how to act in ways that avoid negative responses, both from their teachers and peers. Neuropsychologist Ronald Federici, Psy.D., explains that children like Billy have to be taught how to act, talk, and interact appropriately, free of defiant and asocial behaviors.[2] They either do not know how to be socially appropriate because of the fear and anxiety or because no one has taught them. He breaks it down to teaching a child the Four L's: language, logic, learning, and listening.

Language. Billy needs help learning social language and how to answer in ways that others can comprehend. He may require help in reframing his answers and learning to say things differently. Instructing Billy on how to use whole sentences and phrases, instead of baby talk and "nonsense" talk, will help him develop his skill of connecting with others. Additionally, Billy must be taught the language of emotions and how to identify feelings while connecting them to feeling words.

> **SURVEY SAYS:**
>
> "School would be better if I had more friends."

There are numerous social language cards and games available through websites such as Linguisystems (www.linguisystems.com), the Critical Thinking Company (www.criticalthinking.com), and

Child's Work/Child's Play (www.childswork.com). These products are designed to help children like Billy learn how to make and keep friends, how to detect and interpret nonverbal communication, and how to understand and appropriately respond to other people's perspectives.

Logic. Billy may have a tendency to live in a "magical world," a maladaptive behavior used to escape from overwhelm and fear. He needs assistance coming back into reality. His responses need to make sense and be logical. Billy needs assistance getting out of looping patterns of speech and into thinking that is sequential and rational.

Learning. Punitive measures traditionally used to teach students lessons will not be effective with Billy. Instead of learning from his past mistakes, he will only sink deeper into fear and overwhelm with these techniques. Billy needs to be shown what responses of his were inappropriate, and not criticized, punished, shamed, or scolded.

For the most part, Billy is not aware of his negative social behaviors. They are not intentional. He simply does not get it. People act according to the way they perceive themselves. Billy's perception of himself is not in reality; he has no understanding as to what he looks like. Billy needs a picture of the "real Billy" painted for him. Role-playing, videotaping, and behavioral rehearsals are effective tools (experiential learning instead of cognitive learning).

It has always been assumed that making friends is a skill that children should learn to do naturally on their own. Andy makes friends fairly easily, but such is not the case for Billy. The inability to form social relationships should be considered equal to a child having a learning difficulty, such as dyslexia. If Andy were dyslexic, he would not be asked to figure out on his own how to stop transposing a "b" to a "d" and vice versa. He would be given assistance to teach his brain how to recognize these symbols correctly.

The same holds true for Billy. Billy needs help in training his brain to properly interpret social cues and facial expressions. When teachers regard Billy's behavior as deliberately disrespectful, they become angry and impatient, which only gets Billy more dysregulated and stressed. The solution is to give Billy understanding and to ensure he gets help in practicing new pro-social behaviors. He needs to practice new responses in order to replace old patterns. "How" to make friends must be demonstrated and role-played for and with him.

Listening. Billy's ability to focus and use appropriate eye contact when engaging with a peer or teacher is very limited. Listening drills that practice keeping focused with appropriate eye contact in the context of a safe relationship with a calm and regulated adult may be required. Additionally, Billy's brain is not wired to "listen" to body language and other nonverbal cues. Billy must be taught how to listen to a person's tone of voice, affect, and body language.

Safety and Security. Creating a safe environment at the social and emotional levels for the Billys of the classroom—and all students for that matter—is an extremely effective way to boost overall academic achievement. Students whose social skills are inept are at a higher risk for academic underachievement. When students feel safe and their anxiety is decreased, they are more able to access their thinking brain—their neocortex.

Safe Base. A student like Billy always needs an "escape hatch." Early experiences of trauma left him with a sensitivity to feeling trapped and helpless. If these feelings are triggered, Billy is likely to

> **SURVEY SAYS:**
>
> "If I had my baby sister at school it would be better."

become reactive and in many cases can go into a panic. Billy needs the option to connect with someone with whom he feels safe. He needs a safe base.

To create a safe base for Billy, he should be matched up with an emotionally attuned and regulated adult in the school, a mentor of sorts. As in playing tag, when children run to base for safety, Billy needs a safe base—someone to seek out for regulation and safety—when he becomes agitated, anxious, or upset so that he does not feel trapped. This person can be anybody in the school. It does not take a trained professional in the field of mental health to sit with a student and simply connect with him. The mentor's role would be to check in with Billy, not to discipline him or talk to him about the way he should or should not be acting. A typical conversation might look like this:

Billy: *"Hi."*
Mentor: *"Hi, Billy. How's it going?"*

Billy:	"Okay."
Mentor:	"It's good to see you. How about you come sit next to me while I finish up this task."
Billy:	"Okay."
Mentor:	"You're going to be okay. Take some deep breaths with me. Just let yourself settle and feel safe again."
Billy:	"Okay."
Mentor:	(Breathing deeply to help Billy settle his system, gives Billy quiet time and sends him a few reassuring glances.)
Billy:	"I hate my teacher."
Mentor:	"Sounds like it's not going so well, huh?"
Billy:	"She picks on me and is ALWAYS correcting me and NEVER gives me a break!"
Mentor:	"That's a tough deal. What else is going on?"
Billy:	"I just can't seem to do anything right. I hate my teacher. I hate this stupid school. I hate this entire world."
Mentor:	"How are you feeling about yourself?"
Billy:	"I hate myself! I'm stupid and I don't know how to do any of the math problems. No matter what, I can't ever get them right!"
Mentor:	"How about you and I talk to your teacher about this after school?"
Billy:	"She won't listen!"
Mentor:	"I'll be there. I'll make sure we can all work this out. Okay?"
Billy:	(Grudgingly) "Okay."
Mentor:	"Okay ... take a few more breaths with me. Shake it out with me. Let's get you ready to go back to class."
Billy:	"Hmmmph."
Mentor:	"Ready? Let me walk you back. There's always a way to work these things out. I want you to get the help you need and not get so frustrated anymore. Alright?"
Billy:	"Okay ... thanks."
Mentor:	"I'll meet you here after school."

The mentor's role is simply to provide emotional space for Billy. The mentor is there to listen, ask inquisitive questions, help Billy process and express, and help him calm down and regulate. Notice in the above conversation, the mentor did not lecture, redirect, try to find a solution, or try to change Billy's thinking. Table 11.2 shows more ways to create emotional space for a student who needs one-on-one support to calm down.

Table 11.2. Tips for creating emotional space

How to Create Emotional Space
• Give acceptance without solving the issue.
• Ask exploratory questions to create a deeper understanding.
• Allow the child to be upset without insisting the child stop being upset.
• Accept that the child's reality may be skewed, and do not try to convince him of a different reality.
• Tolerate the negative and exaggerated feelings the child is expressing for the moment in order to help him calm down.
• Give understanding to the child's issue but not necessarily agree with it.
• Be kind, loving, safe, and patient.
• Listen with no agenda of teaching a life lesson. Simply listen. The life lesson will come afterward.
• Validate the child's struggle without identifying what he needs to do differently. That will come later when the child is calm, regulated, and ready for change.
• Engage in the conversation but do not force or insist on answers. Let it unfold naturally.
• Focus on the relationship. Strive for emotional safety and stay regulated. Trust in the process.

No More Survival of the Fittest. Children must learn interpersonal skills and how to solve conflicts to succeed in life. However, the letting children "work it out on their own" approach can be severely damaging to children like Billy. Andy can work through social dilemmas with only minor emotional hardship, but Billy will likely sink further into a state of dysregulation, and negative behaviors will manifest more intensely.

The Billys of the classroom are acutely aware of how they do not fit in and how different they are. This creates a negative self-perception along with more insecurity in the school environment. Social conflicts are opportunities for these students to learn how to improve their social skills instead of increasing their sense of not fitting into the world, and they need teachers to step in and help navigate. Billy lives in a world he does not understand and in a world that does not understand him. He deserves guidance in understanding the nuances of human interactions rather than being left to his own devices and then punished.

> **SURVEY SAYS:**
>
> "Teachers should be aware of kids fighting and not be afraid to interact and do something."

Helping children who are struggling and tussling with each other does not mean handling the conflict through power, control, and pure authority. This will automatically create a divisive dynamic of "me against you" for Billy. His ability to take responsibility will be greatly decreased, as Billy will resist and blame the teacher for the issue. Sending Billy to a time-out or isolative type of punishment to think about what he "did wrong" will only give Billy more time to think about how to "get away with it better next time" or how "stupid" he is and how he "just doesn't fit into this world."

Approaching student conflicts with a level of acceptance, knowing that these students do not have the social maturity or wisdom to know how to do it differently, can keep the teacher in a regulated and mindful framework. Giving compassion and understanding to each student, allowing each student to have a voice, will work to de-escalate the situation.

Instead of punishing and isolating the student who appears to be the instigator, this student requires more direct one-on-one assistance to help him return to a place of regulation. The most out-of-control student is feeling the most isolative and the most threatened; he is the one in the deepest fear state. Children act out from a state of dysregulation and fear. Giving this student attention does not reward his behavior; it teaches him how to change and it stops him from further decompensating. Here is an example from an elementary class:

The students were having "center time." Billy was playing with the math manipulatives and another student when all of a sudden, he began arguing and yelling. The other student just as quickly lost self-control and yelled back. The argument became more heated and Billy continued to elevate the disagreement. Instead of the teacher sending Billy to time-out or sending him to the corner, the teacher first said to the other student, "Andy, Billy isn't feeling very safe right now and I know this doesn't make you feel good being treated this way. Stay here and continue playing while I help Billy. I'll be back to make sure you get what you need also." The teacher calmly took Billy's hand and said, "Let's go over to my desk so I can help you. You're not in trouble, Billy. I just want to make sure you're okay."

Once Billy is calmed down and away from the stressful situation, the teacher can then work with him individually or, in this case, with the entire class. Mantras in the classroom in this particular example would be exceptionally helpful. The teacher could have the entire class stop at their centers and point to the mantra poster board saying, "Class, when you need help, who do you ask?" And the class reads and responds, "We ask the teacher." The teacher reinforces that it is her job to make sure everyone is safe and that there will be no fighting, arguing, or hurting. She points to the mantra poster board again and says, "There will be no what?" And the class responds, "No fighting, no arguing, no hurting."

Practicing problem-solving skills will ensure fewer conflicts in the future. In this way, students learn how to take responsibility for their actions instead of blaming and shunning others for their actions, which typically happens when they are simply punished. They also start learning the vital life skill of self-regulation.

If you are thinking, "But shouldn't Billy get a consequence for his behavior?" consider that he did. Billy was removed from the activity. He essentially had a time-out—only it was with the teacher to give him a chance to learn how to calm his nervous system down. If the teacher feels that Billy should have more of a consequence, she could simply say to Billy, "I need you to stay with me for the rest of center time. We have to learn to be safe in this class, so stay with me and we can try center time again tomorrow."

Billy still receives a "consequence," but the delivery is "we" focused, thereby taking the shame, blame, and punishment out yet removing him from the activity. Billy receives the support he needs, is given a better solution for how to handle himself next time, and is given hope of tomorrow being a better day.

> ### SURVEY SAYS:
> ---
> "Make kids stop bullying me."
>
> "Teachers should make people feel good in the class and not bullied."

No Tolerance for Bullying. Bullying is social issues on steroids. Children like Billy are poignant targets for bullying and it should never be tolerated—ever. Every child has a right to feel safe in school, always.

The U.S. Department of Health & Human Services reports, "Children with disabilities—such as physical, developmental, intellectual, emotional, and sensory disabilities—are at an increased risk of being bullied. Any number of factors—physical vulnerability, social skill challenges, or intolerant environments—may increase the risk."[3] This describes Billy exactly. His deficits and disabilities make him appear weaker and thus easily dominated and mistreated.

When Billy, with a high sensitivity to feeling powerless, hopeless, and helpless, is bullied, he will go into a severe fight-or-flight response. Bullying affects Billy at the primal level. He is likely to become either aggressive and assaultive or he will go to the other end of the spectrum and become depressed or even suicidal. Billy is ill-equipped to handle such intense feelings and he absolutely needs the help and intervening actions of an educator to step forward on his behalf. If not, the results have tragic potential. Here is a story of one mother whose son with a developmental disability was bullied:

> *Last year, there was a group of girls calling my son, a sixth grader, a "retard." The teacher knew about it and made mention of it to the girls but did not follow through on stopping the bullying from that point. When I discussed the situation with the teacher, her response was, "It's just the way teenage girls are. They don't mean anything by it." I took my concerns higher up the ladder and spoke with the administrative staff. I was told that my son simply needed to have a stronger backbone. It was almost as if I did not present a strong enough case of bullying and that this situation was not worthy enough to be considered "legitimate bullying," similar to Todd Akin using the term "legitimate rape." Rape is rape. Bullying is bullying. They are unacceptable, always. My son, due to his traumatic history, is highly sensitive to stress and has an extremely low sense of self. The bullying by this group of girls sent him spiraling downward. As the bullying continued, and no one would take the impact of this on my son seriously, the situation only intensified and he attempted suicide. He went into an extreme flight mode and attempted to create his own exit strategy by killing himself. Fortunately, my son's attempt proved unsuccessful and he is still with us today.*

The traditional justifications for bullying such as the ones given in the story above, along with sayings such as "boys will be boys" or "that's just the way teenagers act," cannot be accepted for any student, especially Billy. With a child like Billy, who has a history of feeling powerless and a belief system in place that says he does not deserve to be on this planet, bullying behavior has to be taken seriously. It has to be stopped by those in charge of the school environment.

Stopping the bullying, however, does not mean putting the bully and the victim into a room and telling them to work it out. These are two Billys who live in survival. One has 100% of the power and the other has zero. The gap is too far for these two to be able to work through a resolution on their own. They need an adult to take strong and immediate action with a no-tolerance policy.

CHAPTER TWELVE

A Program for Billy

■

In order to be irreplaceable, one must always be different.
~ Coco Chanel

E ven when all the parameters to support Billy's learning have been put into place, as described in the previous chapters, Billy may still need a more individualized program. His thinking is so vastly different from Andy's. Two basic options parents and educators have for Billy are the Individual Education Program (IEP) and the 504 Plan.

Individual Education Program. The IEP is a written document developed to meet the individual needs of an eligible student. In simple terms, it is written on an annual basis in compliance with the Individuals with Disabilities Education Act (IDEA) and is federally funded. It is developed by a committee consisting of teachers, school and district administrators, parents/guardians, and anyone else connected to the child whose knowledge of the child will benefit the planning of the IEP. Theoretically, each person on the committee has an equal opportunity to provide input and decision making power within the committee.

In an IEP meeting, the committee looks at the student's present levels of performance, reviews his records, evaluates data and any other relevant information available, and crafts an appropriate plan. The plan will consist of measurable goals and objectives, accommodations, and modifications. The goal is to "level the playing field" for this student so that he can achieve his potential.

To be eligible for an IEP, the child's disability must have an educational impact and the child will have had to been evaluated by a professional, either someone with the school system or an independent evaluator. Typical disabilities for a child like Billy that will qualify him for an IEP include having autism, a developmental delay, an emotional disturbance, a specific learning disability, a processing disorder, and/or a speech or language impairment.

504 Plan. In some situations, a child may not meet the more stringent requirements of an IEP but still needs special accommodations due to a documented condition that adversely affects his educational progress. In such cases, a 504 plan can be an effective and supportive solution. Like the IEP, the 504 Plan is also written by a committee but the plan is much simpler. Its goal is to provide accommodations, services, and modifications the student needs in order for him to have the same advantages as his classmates. The 504 Plan originated with the compliance Federal Rehabilitation Act of 1973, Section 504, but unlike the IEP, the federal government does not directly fund these accommodations. Compliance and accountability are overseen by the Office of Civil Rights.

Traditional View

Traditionally, individualized programs for students have been exceptionally behaviorally based. These programs have worked to manage a student's behaviors through consequences, rewards, and time-outs. The following IEP statement reflects this behavioral management framework:

> *"The teacher will utilize time-outs when misbehavior(s) occur and will reward student with added tokens when appropriate behaviors occur."*

Traditional approaches have also advocated for teachers to use positive reinforcement to promote good behavior. Simultaneously, teachers are encouraged to use planned ignoring responses to avoid reinforcing bad behavior, as well as use immediate consequences to extinguish bad behavior. For example, this statement from an IEP reflects this approach:

"Appropriate, constant, and direct consequences should be given for student's choices. Good choices should be rewarded and bad choices should have an immediate consequence."

Attempts at creating motivation have been through external incentives and "things" students can work toward to earn something. Below are two examples:

"At the end of each week, if student has earned 10 stars, he will be eligible to select a toy out of the teacher's prize box."

"Teacher and parent will increase rewards for work completion and for positive pro-social behavior(s)."

With these behavior management parameters, the question these programs are striving to answer is the traditional question, "How do I get Billy to change his behavior?" Additionally, these programs are implemented only after the student demonstrates negative behaviors, thus they are inherently reactive instead of proactive. They are working to change a behavior that has already been in existence.

The effectiveness of these IEPs is measured by outcomes based on the student's behaviors. They are performance-based programs; the process holds little to no weight, and the process oftentimes goes completely unacknowledged—the sole focus is the measurable and quantifiable outcome.

Traditionally, the goals and objectives in these programs are written with an individual focus. The onus is placed almost entirely on the student to modify his behavior, without explicit parameters that the teacher needs to put into place as well.

New View

When considering all the information presented in this book, it becomes clear that the traditional approach will not work for Billy. In fact, it will most likely increase Billy's negative behaviors. An entirely opposite approach, based on an understanding of how trauma impacts a child's system, needs to be used when developing individual programs for children like Billy. Table 12.1 compares behavioral thinking (traditional view) with regulatory thinking (new view).

Table 12.1. Comparison of behavioral thinking and regulatory thinking

Comparison of Approaches to Individualized Programs	
Traditional View	**New View**
Consequence based	Regulatory based
Rewards and incentives create motivation	Relational influence creates motivation
External controls (point and star charts, detention, removal of privileges)	Internal controls (sense of self, sense of accomplishment, self-acceptance, self-love)
Time-outs	Time-ins
Expectations based on chronological age	Expectations based on emotional/social age
Behavior management	Stress management
Individual focus	Community/family focus
Performance/outcome based	Process based
Intervention	Prevention
Major transitions identified	All transitions identified
Child to fit into the environment	Environment to fit the child
Behavior is a matter of choice	Stress drives behavior

Billy needs a program that will address the question, "What is driving this child's behavior?" It needs to be based on addressing his regulation, not his behavior. Relational influence needs to replace rewards and incentives, which will only set him up for failure. Since Billy is living out of a negative belief system, the plan needs to help him reprogram these beliefs with ways to build his sense of self, sense of accomplishment, and self-acceptance.

Stressful factors that trigger Billy's behavior in his environment must be identified and accommodations made accordingly. This will help to create an environment that fits Billy's high sensitivity to stress and will work in a proactive, preventative way. When understanding how stress plays a key role in Billy's regulation, solutions that involve time-ins, transitional support, and a decrease in stimulation should be written into Billy's plan. Here is the true account of one mom's experience with her Billy:

I was called into a meeting for my son, Billy, who was in the eighth grade at the time. The teachers were pointing out all the bad choices Billy was making and all the negative behaviors he was exhibiting. The behavioral logs were sitting on the table and I asked if we could take a look not at the actual behaviors but what preceded the behaviors—to look at what happened BEFORE Billy became disruptive. In every incident, Billy's behaviors were a reaction to a feeling of being unheard, misunderstood, blamed, or powerless. There was a definite pattern taking place that needed to be addressed rather than simply identifying Billy as a disruptive child who "needed to get his act together" (as one of the teachers put it). Once the pattern was addressed and Billy was helped in learning to appropriately deal with these feelings, his negative behaviors ended.

Words Matter. Let's take a closer look at the wording of traditional IEPs before examining how regulatory concepts can be incorporated into the language of IEPs. Linguistics goes beyond the actual words; it is about the meaning and feeling behind the communication. One's words indicate the mindset and framework from which the communication originates.

It is clear from examples of traditional IEPs and behavioral programs that there is an unsettling judgmental stance toward children like Billy. There is a lack of acceptance that Billy's behaviors are normal—normal based on his life experiences. These behaviors are normal due to the physiological and emotional effects of trauma. A nonacceptance attitude is both directly and indirectly present in the choice of words used in describing behaviors. The following list presents actual statements taken from IEPs along with an explanation as to why the statements are not only negative but damaging to the understanding of the student.

1. *"The student's <u>attention-seeking behavior</u> results in frequently interrupting the teacher, averaging ten times daily."*

   The term "attention-seeking behavior" has traditionally been used to define negative actions. This term misses the point: that children seek attention because they need attention ... they seek it for regulation, acceptance, and love. Therefore, any form of attention they receive is love, positive or negative. This need is not a negative behavior; it is a natural occurrence in any child. The statement could better convey the real issue by stating, "Student frequently seeks regulatory assistance through maladaptive behavioral communications."

2. *"Student's <u>poor</u> social problem-solving skills result in inter-student conflicts."*

   "Poor" is a judgmental word that leads to a misunderstanding about the student. A child with "poor" social skills is a child who missed the needed attention and appropriate early childhood experiences. To be more accurate, this statement could read, "Student's underdeveloped social problem-solving skills result in inter-student conflicts."

3. *"Student's poor <u>anger management skills</u> result in acting-out behaviors." [Student in this example was seven years old.]*

   Children are emotional beings and have a limited capacity to handle their emotions. They are not little adults. The term "anger management" is an adult term being imposed onto a child, with underdeveloped coping skills with an expectation of a skill far beyond his years. He has not yet learned how to self-regulate because he has not had enough positive experiences to learn this mature skill. Thus, it is a regulatory issue, not a behavioral issue. This statement should more accurately be worded, "Student's compromised and underdeveloped self-regulatory skills result in acting-out behaviors."

4. *"Student will <u>escape</u> the demands of circle time and other structured activities."*

Dictionary.com defines "escape" as "to get away," as in "to escape from jail'" and "to avoid a threatening evil."[1] The combative tone of the IEP statement shown here describing a child's behavior is certain to have a grossly negative impact on the teacher-student relationship. There is always a reason for a child's behavior, and in this instance the reason is clearly stated—the "demands" of the activity are too much for the child. Stress and overwhelm are driving this child's resistance. There is nothing criminal about that. This student's behavior could more accurately be described as, "Student becomes overwhelmed and slips into flight mode by the demands of circle time and other structured activities."

5. *"Student <u>avoids</u> the demands of activities that he finds demanding by resisting or withdrawing."*

The word "avoid" has a negative connotation in our culture. If someone tries to avoid you, he is being rude and shallow. Besides being a negative choice of words, this statement offers no understanding as to what is happening to this student internally when he is asked to participate in demanding activities. The use of the word "avoids" offers judgment of him being a problem student. This statement would offer more understanding to this child if revised to, "Student becomes overwhelmed by demanding activities and seeks to self-soothe by resisting or withdrawing."

6. *"Prepare classmates by explaining that student <u>does not know how</u> to appropriately greet them."*

When children are unable to use appropriate social manners, many times this is due to feeling insecure, scared of being rejected, and overwhelmed in group settings. This is a fear-induced behavior. The wording in this statement creates an inharmonious classroom of "us" who know how verses "him" who does not know how. A community/family approach would serve to effectively address the underlying issue of fear and foster a united classroom: "Prepare classmates by explaining that student needs the support of everyone in the class to feel safe and secure."

7. *"The student's acting-out behavior results in frequent <u>violations</u> of classroom rules throughout the day."*

The term "violations" is often associated with the phrase "to violate the law." If someone violates the law, he is a criminal. A student in a classroom may not be following the rules, but in no uncertain terms does he deserve to be associated, even indirectly, with a person who commits a crime. Yet the wording of this statement offers this type of free association. It leaves little room for compassion and relationship from educators interacting with the student, especially during times when he is dysregulated, precisely the times he needs connection and relationship the most. Rewording this statement to the truth would be, "Student is frequently unable to adhere to classroom rules due to overwhelm, stress, and dysregulation."

Judgmental words and phrases lead to a decrease in compassion and understanding. They put up a wall in any relationship and the teacher-student relationship is no exception. Using this type of language with Billy is exceptionally damaging, as he is precisely the student who needs an ever-present amount of understanding, acceptance, and emotional safety. Focus on the words—they need to foster compassion.

The Problem Unveils the Solution. When a student's behaviors can be observed objectively, without judgment and without expecting him to be like Andy, the solution often piggybacks the problem. It takes observing Billy's behaviors through the lens of trauma and asking the right question for this to become visible. The more Billy's behaviors are viewed from the perspective of trauma instead of being judged as bad behavior, the more Billy's behavior simply "makes sense."

Behavior is a form of communication; it communicates what is driving the behavior. If you know what is driving the behavior, the solution becomes clear. The following list gives examples of pulling the solution directly out of the observed behavior. The italicized statements come directly from behavioral assessments of students. A discussion on how this observation unveils the solution follows.

1. *"If pushed to participate, Billy will react by throwing objects, screaming, or stating, 'Shut up.'"*

   Feelings of being powerless will ignite when Billy is "pushed to participate." The feeling of being controlled and powerless is a trauma trigger for Billy. For Billy to participate without reacting, he will need to be encouraged, supported, and assisted—all of this with an adult with whom he has a safe and strong relationship.

2. *"During activities that are particularly demanding for Billy, he may show increased rigidity about favorite activities, objects, play routines, and conversations."*

   When Billy faces challenging and demanding tasks, he will typically decompensate. He becomes overwhelmed and in his attempt to find stability and regulation, he will revert back to activities that are familiar. Hence, in this example, Billy's need for what is familiar and what feels good and safe is increased. He becomes inflexible and rigid simply because he is seeking safety. The solution would be to chunk demanding tasks into smaller amounts, give Billy reassurance when he becomes noticeably distressed, and tolerate his rigidity in the short term in order for him to feel secure.

3. *"Billy disengages in class particularly <u>during large-group</u> activities."*

When children have an early history of neglect, they typically have an overly developed ability to dissociate, meaning they can disconnect and disengage from reality when life becomes too much. They may appear to be daydreamers, zoned out in their own worlds. In the classroom, when this Billy gets overwhelmed by the complexity of social dynamics created within a large group, his system goes into automatic pilot and the shut-off valve activates. Complex social dynamics confuse and frustrate him. The solution is for Billy to remain in only small-group settings for now, or when in large groups Billy will receive direct support from the teacher or another adult. When he can regulate off another adult during large-group activities, he will learn over time how to stay present, instead of disengaging automatically.

Teachers. The traditional individualized program has focused solely on how the student can change, what the student needs to do differently, and how the student can take a greater amount of responsibility. In the past, 100% of the responsibility and accountability was placed on Billy, without recognizing that there are two sides to the teacher-student coin. The teacher's ability to either respond or react has a greater influence than any other variable in the student's life. Too much energy has been wasted on designing programs that use point charts, token rewards, and privileges while the greatest influential factor has literally been right in front of the classroom the entire time.

If Billy is working to change his behavior but is still struggling and demonstrating some negative behavior, the ultimate outcome will be greatly determined by the way the teacher handles Billy. If the teacher yells and rigidly demands that Billy modify his behavior, Billy will most likely not show improvement. Fear does not help a child like Billy. However, if the teacher is regulated and shows strength through compassion and understanding, Billy has a much greater chance of improving. Unfortunately, this dynamic is rarely identified in the goal statements for Billy in an IEP, and the expectations of the teacher in helping to implement these goals is rarely identified.

In the following list, examples of actual goals written for students on their IEPs are given. While these goals are reasonable, they are based solely on Billy making a modification, without explicit directions for how the teacher needs to respond for Billy to achieve this goal. Flipping the coin to the other side, questions are then posed to consider what Billy would need from his teacher to fully accomplish the goal.

1. *"Student will verbalize and express his feelings when becoming agitated."*

    - Can the adult in this dyad hold the emotional space for Billy to accomplish this goal?
    - If Billy is expressing his feelings, is he met with acceptance, validation, and tolerance from the adult? Or is he being lectured to, controlled, or invalidated? Is he told, "Well, you shouldn't feel that way because you had your turn earlier—you have to learn to wait your turn"?

2. *"Student will use verbal greetings with eye contact each morning, as measured by observation and data collection."*

    - Is the teacher taking care of herself and making certain that internally she is in a state of calm and love? What is the level of her heart coherence (as discussed in chapter 9)?
    - Is the teacher being perceived as inviting to the student through her body language and other nonverbal communication? Does the student perceive her as a safe base in order to feel safe enough to make eye contact with her?

3. *"Student will respond in a calm manner when consequences are administered by an adult x out of y times, as measured by data collection."*

- When these consequences are being handed to the student, what is the tone of the delivery? Are nonblaming or blaming words being used?
- Is the teacher projecting any of her frustration onto the student, either directly or indirectly?
- Is there equality in the level of consequence to the level of misbehavior, and does the consequence truly work to teach a lesson or is the consequence simply a punishment?

4. *"Student to utilize strategies to relieve stress and anxiety (either by himself or with teacher's assistance) so to not harm himself or others."*

- If the student is receiving assistance from the teacher, will the teacher be mindful enough to make certain she is regulated and calm, making certain she is not adding more stress and anxiety into the dynamic with the student?
- Is the teacher self-validating and confident enough not to take it personally if the student is unable to calm down even when she is helping him?

When questions such as these are addressed and Billy is given the relational responses he needs, Billy's ability to successfully accomplish these goals will increase significantly.

Parents. Billy functions best in environments that are consistent and predictable. When parents and teachers work together to support Billy both at school and at home in a coherent fashion, Billy feels safer, is more regulated, and has more space for academic achievement. Congruency between home and school environments provides an external structure that helps him work to his highest potential.

Billy's individualized programs should always include parameters for developing this consistency between Billy's parent(s) and his teacher(s). The following list presents strategies for teachers and parents to coordinate their efforts:

1. *Teacher will summarize and send by email the student's regulation and stress levels at school in order to support student's recovery at home.*

2. *Parent will email a brief written report to the teacher on the child's stress level at home, as well as any home events that may affect the student's behavior at school.*

3. *Teacher will give information to families about upcoming projects and deadlines (that may prove overwhelming for the student) to provide home support for the student.*

4. *Parent will share with the teacher strategies that have proven successful at home in order to provide consistency in both environments for the student.*

5. *Parent will be available during the day to help regulate student through phone calls, text messages, and lunch visits.*

6. *Parent will drop student off at school in the morning in as much a regulated state as possible. When the student is having a difficult morning, parent will notify the teacher at the start of the school day to prepare the teacher.*

7. *Parent and teacher will stay in close communication by email and phone to discuss future school events that are not within the normal classroom routine (class assemblies, teacher absence, field trips, etc.).*

Implementation. As the saying goes, "It's all in the delivery." This holds true for delivering an individualized program to a student. When a student has an IEP, he may automatically feel different and "less than" his classmates. He may also feel the IEP is a punishment for being "bad," since it most likely came about after he was in trouble numerous times.

The program needs to be reviewed and discussed with the student. The delivery to the student needs to be in the framework that the "adults met to find a way to help you and support you" and that the "adults met to figure out how to help you feel safe and secure at school." Too often, the delivery is quite the opposite—that the "adults had to meet to find a way to get you to behave."

When Billy can see that the plan is in place for his benefit, the threat is removed and the fear of being a bad student is minimized. It needs to be presented as a plan that is being done for him, not to him.

Examples. There really cannot be a formula or prototype used when creating an individualized program for a student (hence, the word "individualized" would be a misnomer). However, to write a program that incorporates the ideas contained in this book, it will be important to train your mind and alter your thinking out of the traditional mindset. The following list provides example statements that could be included in an IEP. Think about how the wording and approach in each statement reflects the ideas presented in this book. Also take note of how the students' responses in the survey give the exact same solutions.

SURVEY SAYS:

"Smaller groups in each class."

"Less distractions."

"More breaks throughout the class."

"One on one with teachers."

"Having fun projects."

"Art, I love art and you can express yourself with art."

"Resting in between."

ACCOMODATIONS
1. Student to have extended time for assignments.
2. Group activities for student to be small (no more than five students).
3. Student to be given frequent breaks during the school day.

4. Learning activities will be broken down into smaller assignments and "chunked" for student so student can see an end to the assignment.

5. Student will be seated next to the teacher.

6. Student will be seated at the back of the classroom behind other students. [This is for a student who has been abused in the past and is afraid of being hurt by someone coming up behind him.]

7. Student to be allowed to sit on fitness ball when doing assignments.

8. Visual and auditory stimuli to be reduced in the classroom by 30%.

9. Student's assignments to be shortened by 50%.

10. Student to be exempt from homework for three months.

11. Student's assignments to be altered to include art, projects, and other creative means of communicating when appropriate.

12. Student to be given time in advance to prepare for transitions to new or different activities.

SURVEY SAYS:

"Give kids enough time. I never have enough time and I get frustrated."

13. Student to be provided adult support to make transitions to new or different activities.

14. Student to be provided advance notice of changes in routines to allow him to prepare for and process these changes.

15. Student to be given alternate periods of sitting with periods of movement.

16. Student to be allowed to use noise-canceling headphones or earplugs when requested.

17. Daily schedule to be posted for the student.

18. Student to carry a visual schedule of his day's routine.

19. Student to be given an extended amount of time for both oral and written responses.

20. Student to be provided more hands-on activities within song and story time to assist student in becoming more engaged.

21. Assignments to be given to student one at a time to avoid work overload.

22. An identified staff to meet student at the bus and escort him to his classroom so that he will enter the classroom more calmly.

23. Student to sit away from distracting stimuli (air conditioner, high-traffic areas, etc.).[2]

24. Student's assignments and work periods to coincide with student's span of attention using the visual aid of a timer.[3]

25. Student to be allowed to stand when working at his desk.[4]

26. Student is not to be assigned large quantities of written work.[5]

> **SURVEY SAYS:**
>
> ---
>
> "More time with tests."

27. Nonwritten forms of work to be accepted by student (i.e., displays, oral reports, projects, posters).[6]

TESTING

1. Testing to be done in a small group and calm setting.

2. Student's tests will not be timed to reduce student's test stress

3. Student to give test responses orally instead of written. (Tests to be administered orally.)

INTERPRETATIONS

1. Escalation signals (playing with pencil, talking out, inappropriate laughing) will be identified as dysregulation, not inappropriate behavior.

2. Student's negative behavior to be recognized as a signal of increased anxiety and stress level.

3. Negative behavior to be recognized as a regulatory issue (rather than a behavioral issue with stress, fear, and overwhelm being the focus) to help student get back on track.

4. A relationship-focused environment will be created for student by using time-ins instead of time-outs.

ASSISTANCE

1. Student to be given strategies (i.e., colored and labeled folders) to improve organizational skills.

2. Student to be provided clear guidelines for getting organized.

SURVEY SAYS:

"What would make me want to get up and go to school is that I know that the teachers are willing to help you with something if you don't understand the assignment."

3. Student to be given a locker near the guidance office and assistance three times a week in keeping the locker organized.

4. Student will be asked individually each morning to turn in his homework.

5. Adult to transcribe verbal responses for written work (schoolwork and/or homework).

6. Student to be given one-on-one attention to understand assignments when needed.

7. Teacher/aide to check in with student often for understanding and to review assignment expectations.

8. Student to be given frequent calm reminder of rules.

9. Student to be given assistance when making transitions between educational tasks and settings.

10. To minimize frustrations and subsequent acting-out behaviors, teacher will provide student with frequent breaks and ongoing encouragement.

11. Student to be reminded to check over his work if performance is rushed.[7]

12. Student to be given assistance in setting short-term goals in completing assignments, especially long-term assignments such as book reports, projects, and research papers.

13. Student not to be penalized for sloppy handwriting. Type-written papers to be accepted.[8]

14. Student to be given assistance when interacting socially when withdrawn.[9]

> **SURVEY SAYS:**
>
> "Teachers who are more hands on with their students. Don't just hand out assignments and lecture; they get more involved with the students."

RELATIONSHIP

1. Student to be given the choice to talk to a preferred adult when unable to stay on task and within classroom rules. Student will be given frequent individual check-ins throughout his day.

2. Student to be given verbal cues with reassurance of security and safety when student becomes agitated and off track.

3. Teachers and staff to provide active listening time to acknowledge student's feelings and to help student build trust in school relationships.

4. Teacher and student to build their relationship outside of school. For instance, if student has a bad day, teacher will call him in the evening to reassure him that things will go better the next day.

5. Student to be a peer teacher to another student in an area where he excels.

BEHAVIOR/REGULATION

1. Student will be given choices when becoming dysregulated:
    - Read a book for ten minutes.
    - Take a walk with an assigned adult.
    - Go to a safe zone in the classroom.
    - Work on the computer for ten minutes.

2. Student to be given self-calming strategies (putty, stress ball, gum, etc.) when negative behaviors are demonstrated.

3. Student will increase his ability to self-regulate by utilizing strategies for self-calming with visual and/or verbal cues.

> **SURVEY SAYS:**
>
> "School would be better not having warning charts."

4. Mantras to be used three times a day to help student develop emotional safety. Examples include:

Teacher: "Who's safe?"
Child: "I am safe."
Teacher: "All of the time or some of the time?"

Child: "All the time!"
Teacher: "Who is in charge to keep you safe?"
Child: "You [the teacher] are in charge to keep me safe."
Teacher: "All of the time or some of the time?"
Child: "All of the time!"

5. Teacher will help student regulate and focus by touching student's shoulder, sitting by student, or signaling student with prearranged signals.

6. Teacher to use touch as a way to help regulate student by placing a hand on the shoulder, taking student by the hand to lead him back to the desk, initiating breathing exercises with student, etc.

> **SURVEY SAYS:**
> _____
>
> "Don't be really controlling (we need flexibility with assignments and encouragement with successes)."

7. Teachers and staff to provide one-on-one time to help student regulate by going for a walk and or getting a drink of water.

8. Student to leave the classroom for assistance with an identified staff person for a "walk, talk, and regulate" session when needed.

9. Student to be offered to move to a pre-identified comfort area when he becomes frustrated. If student becomes upset and needs a break, teacher to remind him that he can go to the comfort area.

10. Student to learn to seek an adult for safety and assistance when transitions or peer negotiations prove difficult.

> **SURVEY SAYS:**
> _____
>
> "If you have something that reminds you of hope such as a rock (small), pen or key chain ... take it along for a reminder."

11. Student to sit near teacher at circle time to help guide and regulate him.

12. Student to be next to a regulated adult while in line with the class.

SURVEY SAYS:

"For 5th grade my best friend helped me through school, so if you have a bud stick close to em."

13. While in line with the class, student to be given a task or job (carry something, "give yourself a hug") to keep him focused and feeling worthy.

14. Student to sit next to a good role model.

15. Student to sit near a "study buddy."[10]

16. Student to be given a checklist of important steps to help him self-monitor his progress. Teacher to provide cues when a step has been missed.[11]

SURVEY SAYS:

"I should be able to eat a snack when I need it."

17. Student to be spoken to in a soft and nonthreatening manner if showing signs of anxiety and dysregulation.

18. Student to be able to have a snack midmorning and midafternoon if requested.

TEACHERS

1. Student's team to be trained about childhood trauma.

SURVEY SAYS:

"I didn't like when the teacher yelled at kids, it made me scared."

2. Adults to approach student from a calm and collected state of mind at all times.

3. Teacher to keep as predictable a schedule as possible.

4. Teachers and staff to avoid power struggles by not insisting that student respond verbally in the heat of the moment but instead allow student time to regulate back down and process with teacher once calm.

5. Teachers and staff to monitor their body language so as to not indirectly communicate negativity to student.

6. Teacher to include a plan for student in her substitute packet. This will include a staff member who can support student if needed along with simple regulatory based de-escalation techniques for the substitute.

PARENTS

1. Meetings with parents will be set up to foster positive collaboration and a consistent plan from home to school.

2. Parent to notify teacher on mornings student will be arriving more dysregulated than is typical.

3. Parent to be available during the school day to check in with student through phone calls and text messaging.

4. Parent to help and encourage student at home to get organized (i.e., set a routine for homework, check backpack with student nightly, help organize materials).

5. Parent to communicate with teacher about student's strengths and interests outside of school.[12]

Epilogue

■

Twelve chapters and almost two hundred pages later of information on how to find understanding and *Help for Billy* should be all that is needed to make things work for Billy. Right? Sometimes yes, but sometimes no. The reality may actually hold a different outcome and the reason comes down to one simple truth: Billy may not be ready to receive this understanding and help.

Ultimately, we have to understand that Billy is on his own journey. He is on his own timetable and his own organic path to healing. Healing takes courage and the ability to break down massive protective barriers, barriers that were created to protect the heart and soul from more overwhelming amounts of pain and fear.

Our work is done after we have provided what has been described in the last twelve chapters' worth of support, understanding, and love. The only step after that is to detach—detach from the outcome. There is nothing more to do at this point. Just detach.

Detachment is hard because we live in a world that is outcome based. Our school systems epitomize outcome-driven structures. Funding, the bottom line for all schools, is determined in most districts by achievement and the outcome of the students. To stay focused on the *process* requires us to find the courage to place confidence in the power of love, to have certainty, beyond a shadow of a doubt, that love will never fail. What has failed us in the past is that fear got in the way and created more disciplinary problems and more resistance from Billy.

We are asking Billy to change and to trust in love; we must do the same. We are asking Billy to let go of his defenses and internal protective forces, thus we must also make these changes in order to complete this process for Billy.

Let go of Billy's outcome. It is not about giving up; it is about letting go and changing the tool of measurement. Ask yourself about the process in which you were engaged with Billy: "Did I give Billy understanding, acceptance, and validation today?" These are the things that should be measured because these are, in reality, the only parts over which you have *any* control. We cannot control the outcome of any child, especially Billy. Thinking that we can is in essence ignoring and discrediting the strength and power of free will.

We are on this planet in a framework of free will, all of us. This is why every one of us is resistant to power and control. We were given this gift to learn and experience what true love is. Each of us is here to migrate back to the essence of our origins—back to the fullness and completeness of unconditional love. For this reason, a controlling and fear-based model within any organization, whether it is a corporation, a personal relationship, or a classroom, will always fail in the long term.

The solution is to flip the evaluation and focus back to us—the teacher, the parent, the administrator, the school support person— because nothing is guaranteed except for the gift of giving love. It is then up to the receiver to receive the love or reject it, to either change or stay the same.

Your ability to give love and stay mindful is the new outcome.

At the end of each day, each year, each decade, or entire lifetime, look back and ask yourself if you did all you could to make a loving and positive difference. We have been asking the wrong questions, which can only lead to feeling utterly unsuccessful. We have been asking whether the child behaved, whether he passed the state achievement test, or whether he was accepted into Harvard. As we have seen throughout this book, if you ask the wrong questions, you'll get the wrong answers.

The questions that each of us working with children should be asking are, "What was my level of love?" and "To what extent was I able to get outside of my own desires and agenda to be able to be in the shoes of Billy?"

When you have been able to fully and unconditionally deliver *Help for Billy*, your work is complete. There is nothing else to do. It is then up to Billy to receive the help and make the needed changes.

Sometimes Billy can change, sometimes he cannot. Or perhaps he simply is not ready to change and it is not the right timing. At this point love is about letting go and stepping back to give Billy his right to free will. There is nothing else to do but love him, create boundaries for him, and continue doing your best because your best is good enough. Let love take over from here and be kind and loving to yourself, always.

Press on,
Heather T. Forbes, LCSW

Notes

■

Chapter 1

[1] Federici, R. S. (2012). Creating safety and healing. *Aggression Training for Families*. Denver, Colorado.

Chapter 2

[1] WebMD (2005). Fetus to mom: You're stressing me out! *WebMD*. Retrieved from http://www.webmd.com/baby/features/fetal-stress

[2] Jones, B. (2010). Stress hormone in womb predicts poorer cognitive development, but loving care can "undo" it. *Medical News Today*. Retrieved from http://www.medicalnewstoday.com/releases/180573.php

[3] WebMD (2005). Fetus to mom: You're stressing me out! *WebMD*. Retrieved from http://www.webmd.com/baby/features/fetal-stress

[4] Ibid.

[5] Perry, B. D. (2012). The impact of trauma & neglect on child development. *Coalition for the Prevention of Child Abuse and Neglect Child Abuse Prevention Awareness 2012 Event*. Colorado Springs, CO.

[6] Schore, A. N. (2008). Affect regulation and the repair of the self: The right hemisphere is dominant in psychotherapy. *Neuroscience Meets Recovery*. Las Vegas, NV.

[7] Scaer, R. C. (2007). *The body bears the burden: Trauma, dissociation, and disease*. New York, NY: Routledge.

[8] Schore, A. N. (2008). Affect regulation and the repair of the self: The right hemisphere is dominant in psychotherapy. *Neuroscience Meets Recovery*. Las Vegas, NV.

9 Bowlby. J. (1988). *A secure base: Parent-child attachment and healthy development.* New York, NY: Basic Books.

10 Kneutgen, J. (1970). A musical form and its biological function: About the effects of lullabies. *Zeitschrift für Experimentelle Angewandte Psychologie, 17,* 245–265.

Chapter 3

1 Schutz, L. E. (2005). Broad-perspective perceptual disorder of the right hemisphere. *Neuropsychology Review, 15*(1), 11–27.

2 Schore, A. N. (2008). Affect regulation and the repair of the self: The right hemisphere is dominant in psychotherapy. *Neuroscience Meets Recovery.* Las Vegas, Nevada.

3 Ibid.

4 James City. (2005, March 5). Police arrest 8-year-old boy after outburst. *The Virginia Gazette.*

Chapter 4

1 Raver, C. C. (2003). *Young children's emotional development and school readiness.* (ERIC Digest No. 16). Retrieved from ERIC database. (EDO-PS-03-8)

Chapter 5

1 Lipton, B. H. (2010). Are you programmed at birth? *Heal Your Life.* Retrieved from http://www.healyourlife.com/author-bruce-h-lipton-phd/2010/08/wisdom/personal-growth/are-you-programmed-at-birth

2 Newberg, A., & Waldman, M. R. (2006). *Why we believe what we believe: Uncovering our biological need for meaning, spirituality, and truth.* New York, NY: Free Press.

3 Ibid.

[4] Ibid.

[5] Federici, R. S. (personal communication, August 18, 2009).

Chapter 6

[1] Hsieh, T. (2010). *Delivering happiness: A path to profits, passion, and purpose*. New York, NY: Business Plus Hachette Book Group.

[2] Ibid.

Chapter 7

[1] Haughey, S. (n.d.). *No more green light, yellow light, red light behavior management plan!* http://fairydustteaching.blogspot. com/2011/01/no-more-green-light-yellow-light-red.html

Chapter 8

[1] Transition. (2012). *Thefreedictionary.com*. Farlex, Inc. Retrieved August 12, 2012, from http://www.thefreedictionary. com/transition

[2] Scaer, R. C. (2005). *The trauma spectrum. Hidden wounds and human resiliency*. New York, NY: W.W. Norton & Company.

[3] Carnegie, D. (2009). *How to win friends and influence people*. New York, NY: Simon & Schuster.

[4] Hypercusis Network. (2012). Decibel guide. Retrieved August 25, 2012, from http://www.hyperacusis.net/hyperacusis/ decibel+guide/default.asp

Chapter 9

[1] Teacher. (2012). *Dictionary.com*. Farlex, Inc. Retrieved July 15, 2012, from http://dictionary.reference.com/browse/teacher

[2] Childre, D. L. & Martin, H. (2000). *The HeartMath solution: The Institute of HeartMath's revolutionary program for engaging the power of the heart's intelligence.* New York, NY: HarperCollins Publishers, Inc.

[3] Schore, A. N. (2008). Affect regulation and the repair of the self: The right hemisphere is dominant in psychotherapy. *Neuroscience Meets Recovery.* Las Vegas, NV.

[4] Prosen, S., Vitulic, H. S., & Skraban, O. P. (2011). Teachers' emotional expression in interaction with students of different ages. *CEPS Journal, 1*(3), 141–157.

Chapter 10

[1] The Franklin Institute. (n.d.). *Stress and memory.* Retrieved August 4, 2008, from http://www.fi.edu/learn/brain/stress.html#stressmemory

[2] Meltz, B. F. (2002, September 19). How parents can help remove homework hurdles. *Boston Globe.* Retrieved from http://www.boston.com/community/moms/articles/2002/09/19/removing_some_of_the_homework_hurdles

[3] Thomas, N. I. (1997). *Teacher resources: Homework.* Retrieved June 4, 2008, from http://www.attachment.org/teachers/homework

[4] Bright Futures. (n.d.). *Homework problems.* Retrieved June 2, 2008, from http://www.brightfutures.org/mentalhealth/pdf/professionals/mc/homework.pdf

[5] MacKenzie, R. J. (2001). *Setting limits with your strong-willed child: Eliminating conflict by establishing clear, firm, and respectful boundaries.* New York: NY: Three Rivers Press.

[6] Meltz, B. F. (2002, September 19). How parents can help remove homework hurdles. *Boston Globe*. Retrieved from http://www.boston.com/community/moms/articles/2002/09/19/removing_some_of_the_homework_hurdles

[7] Ibid.

[8] Arnsten, A. F. (1998). Development of the cerebral cortex: XIV. Stress impairs prefrontal cortical function. *American Academy of Child Adolescent Psychiatry, 37*(12): 1337–1339.

[9] Frean, A. (2008, March 11). Homework for primary pupils should be scrapped. (2008). *The Times*. Retrieved June 8, 2008, from http://www.timesonline.co.uk/tol/news/uk/education/article3525626.ece

[10] Kohn, A. (2007, January/February). *Rethinking homework*. Retrieved August 31, 2012, from http://www.alfiekohn.org/teaching/rethinkinghomework.htm

[11] Bowlby. J. (1988). *A secure base: Parent-child attachment and healthy development.* New York, NY: Basic Books.

[12] MacKenzie, R. J. (2001). *Setting limits with your strong-willed child: Eliminating conflict by establishing clear, firm, and respectful boundaries.* New York: NY: Three Rivers Press.

Chapter 11

[1] Wikipedia (2012). Albert Mehrabian. Retrieved from http://en.wikipedia.org/wiki/Albert_Mehrabian

[2] Federici, R. S. (2003). *Help for the hopeless child: A guide for families.* Alexandria, VA: Dr. Ronald S. Federici and Associates.

[3] U.S. Department of Health & Human Services. (2012). Bullying and youth with disabilities and special health needs. Retrieved from http://www.stopbullying.gov/at-risk/groups/special-needs/index.html

Chapter 12

[1] Escape. (2012). *Dictionary.com*. Farlex, Inc. Retrieved July 25, 2012, from http://dictionary.reference.com/browse/escape

[2] Federici, R. S. (2003). *Help for the hopeless child: A guide for families.* Alexandria, Virginia: Dr. Ronald S. Federici and Associates.

[3] Ibid.

[4] Ibid.

[5] Ibid.

[6] Ibid.

[7] Ibid.

[8] Ibid.

[9] Ibid.

[10] Ibid.

[11] Ibid.

[12] Ibid.

Index

∎

About The Author

■

Heather T. Forbes, LCSW

Heather T. Forbes, LCSW, is the co-founder and owner of the Beyond Consequences Institute in Boulder, Colorado. Forbes has worked in the field of trauma and healing since 1999. She is an internationally published author on the topics of raising children with difficult and severe behaviors, the impact of trauma on the developing child, adoptive motherhood, and self-development. Coming from a family of educators, Forbes has a heart for children in the classroom and for finding ways to teach the child who seems "unteachable." Her signature style is to bridge the gap between scientific research and real-life application to equip parents, educators, and therapists with practical and effective tools. Much of her experience and insight on understanding trauma, disruptive behaviors, and adoption-related issues comes from her direct mothering experience of her two adopted children and mentoring of a severly traumatized young adult.